David

W. Phillip Keller

David

I

The Time of Saul's Tyranny

WORD BOOKS
PUBLISHER
WACO, TEXAS

A DIVISION OF
WORD, INCORPORATED

Library of Congress Cataloging in Publication Data

Keller, W. Phillip (Weldon Phillip), 1920–
    David, the time of Saul's tyranny.

    1. David, King of Israel.   2. Saul, King of Israel.
3. Palestine—Kings and rulers—Biography.   4. Bible.
O.T.—Biography.   I. Title.
BS580.D3K43   1985   222'40924 [B]   85-6265
ISBN 0-8499-0470-6

Printed in the United States of America

To those precious men and women
across the country
who
pray for me every day

A Note of Appreciation

First of all my gratitude goes to Mr. Al Bryant, Managing Editor of Word Books, who long ago invited me to undertake this work. He has waited patiently for it to come to life. His encouragement and good cheer have been an inspiration in the writing.

Miss Linda Sue Lambright was gracious in undertaking to type the manuscript at a time when my wife was unable to do so. Her skill and efficiency have been such a help.

The prayers and enthusiasm of God's people for this project have been an inspiration. Morning by morning there has been an acute awareness of Christ's presence directing the endeavor.

Contents

The steps of a good man are ordered by the Lord:
and he delighteth in his way.
Though he fall, he shall not be utterly cast down:
for the Lord upholdeth him with his hand.

Psalm 37:23–24
(*Written by David*)

About This Book

The life of David, Israel's second king, holds enormous fascination for people everywhere. Somehow he attracts the attention of both Christian and non-Christian. There is a certain charisma about his character that commands the interest of both adults and children. His exploits and daring are woven into the colorful tapestry of a brilliant career.

So it is not surprising that scholars, historians, writers, painters and film producers have directed their time and skill to David. Perhaps this explains why during the past five years three different publishers have urged me to do a study of his life.

Because the biblical record concerning this man is so extensive at first I considered this assignment almost too formidable. Finally it was decided the work should be done in stages, embracing more than one volume. This book is the first of those works.

Customarily, my main thrust in dealing with a biblical character is to discover the purposes of God in the record. Why did the Almighty choose and use this person to achieve His ends in the earth scene? What were the divine principles at work in this life used to lift an individual to notoriety above his people? Are there spiritual lessons we can learn from him?

This book is not just a historical narrative of David's life. Nor is it intended to be a somber, scholarly exposition of his exploits. Rather, it is a devotional study of what our Lord can do with a man who, though terribly tough and passionate, has a purpose to do God's will.

As with my previous books on Joshua, Gideon and Elijah, the emphasis lies upon the personal response of the person's spirit to the Lord. Herein lies the secret to the subsequent success or failure of that individual to walk with God in supernatural ways.

Put in the terms of the New Testament we are told plainly that *"all these things happened to them as examples, and they were written for our admonition, on whom the ends of the ages have come"* (1 Corinthians 10:11 NKJV).

It is inevitable, of course, that in depicting the life of David, one must deal also with the other leading characters of his time. He must be seen in blazing contrast with Saul, Israel's first awful king. We must understand his friendship with Jonathan, the first prince in Israel. The part played by women in his life is extraordinary. His interaction with the men under his command is fascinating. His respect for the prophets and priests of the Most High startles us.

Most important, David's devotion to God touches us deeply.

As an author I have sought carefully to include in this work only that which God's gracious Spirit intended. Every effort has been made to set the stage and follow the scriptural record as accurately as possible. All of the material in this work was first used in active Bible study sessions with eager people anxious to discover fresh truth from God's Word. So this book is not a theological treatise compiled in an ivory tower environment.

Rather it has emerged from months and months of study, prayer, meditation and active interaction with groups of keen Christians. It bears the dynamic thrust of real life situations in which most of us can find personal identification. Saul, David and Jonathan are not plastic characters separate from our humanity. They are blood and bone and breath, with our same inner struggles of spirit and soul.

It has moved me deeply to see and sense the profound impact these studies have made on the lives of those who came to the classes. Men and women have met the living God in fresh and wondrous ways as we saw Him at work in the days of David.

The same truth so powerful then has not altered. It transcends time, cultures and human personalities. The same God Almighty stands ready today to do His own profound work in the lives of His people. May this book be used to produce great characters of shining worth for His reputation and pleasure.

David

1

Israel Demands a King

Three hundred and eighty years had passed since the exciting night of Israel's *Exodus* from Egypt. In power and moving majesty God had delivered His own peculiar, chosen people of the covenant out of slavery to the Pharaohs. With a mighty hand He had moved them across the Red Sea and into the desert shadows of Sinai.

Under the guidance of magnificent men like Moses and Joshua, Israel had traversed the wilderness, crossed the flooding Jordan and settled in Canaan. There they drove out the Amorites and partitioned Palestine for their own permanent homeland.

It was our God's clear intention that Israel should be an unusual human society. They were to be neither a democracy nor a monarchy, but a *theocracy* in which He Himself was paramount. For spiritual leadership Israel would look to the priests drawn from the tribe of Levi. For civil jurisdiction they would be led by judges.

For 340 dismal years, after the death of the illustrious Joshua, Israel stumbled and staggered under various leaders . . . some good, others deplorable. Invaded frequently by their old enemies, plundered and oppressed by their neighboring nations, the people of Israel became rebellious and discontented with God's divine arrangement for their government.

Finally, in grim determination to make a change, the people came to Samuel demanding a king. The aged judge, also considered a prophet of the Most High, was aghast at Israel's audacity. Never before had this peculiar people shown such a determination to have a monarch of their own. At any cost they would establish a royal family to lead them.

In part this violent action was triggered by Samuel's own wayward sons. He had appointed them as judges to succeed him. But their propensity to corruption and their perversion of justice enraged the people. So they insisted on a king.

In deep remorse Samuel sought the counsel of God. The reassurance which came to the dear old veteran was that Israel was not rejecting him but rather rejecting the government of Jehovah God. Samuel was to warn them of their folly, yet accede to their wishes.

It was a crucial turning point in Israel's tragic history. It was the hinge upon which all of her future would turn for the next 370 years. It was the precise midway point between the *Exodus* from Egypt with its slavery, back into abysmal bondage to the Babylonians.

In moving entreaty Samuel warned his people of the perilous path they were choosing, contrary to God's will. He described in vivid detail the era of tyranny that would overtake them under the king of their choice. They would cry out in anguish because of his abuse.

Samuel's warnings were of no avail. Instead, Israel demanded even more vehemently that they be given a king who would rule their territory and fight their battles.

In this way they were sure they could become an equal force against their adversaries.

What Israel had done as a nation, the great majority of us do as individuals. We insist on having our own way. We adamantly exercise our own wills in rejecting the government of God in our own lives. We are determined to control our own conduct. We choose to be kings in our own careers. We blatantly reject the King of Glory and refuse to submit to the sovereignty of His gracious Spirit.

This is a most dangerous course of action.

The results of our rebellion can be devastating.

Yet God, very God, rather than override our wills, grants us what we insist upon. Often, the consequences are catastrophic for us and grievous to Him.

This was to be the case for Israel in the choice of Saul as their first king. A man of magnificent physique and impressive appearance, Saul was selected for his sheer physical strength. Combined with his handsome features was a formidable will, strong as steel.

This becomes quickly apparent when he sets out to search for the asses that strayed from his father's herd. Saul was not content merely to look around the neighbor's pastures for the missing animals. No, indeed, he and his servant tramped close to a hundred miles across the rocky ranges of the surrounding territory determined to find the donkeys.

Nor was this enough. If necessary he would even seek out Samuel and consult with the veteran seer to obtain divine direction in his search. Quite obviously he had never seen Samuel before, never felt any need of his spiritual advice. But when it came to donkeys nothing would deter him. He would even pay solid silver for the prophet's services.

When the two men met Samuel, he was unknown to them. The grizzled old man of God had to identify himself to the spiritually dull young men. And, no doubt, when the prophet pronounced that Saul was to be Israel's new monarch the news was a bit more than he could manage to grasp. After all, asses were the younger man's foremost interest in life just now, and who wanted to be a king over his countrymen when he would be much more contented caring for donkeys?

Samuel hastened to assure the handsome young Hercules towering over him that in fact his asses had been found. The venerable old prophet urged Saul to set aside all further concern for the donkeys. Instead, he entreated him to take seriously the new honors and responsibilities his role as king would embrace . . . especially a monarch in Israel!

Rather lamely and somewhat shamefully Saul protested that he came from the smallest tribe in Israel—Benjamin. He pointed out that his family was not prominent, but rather the least in his community. Why then should he be chosen? He had hoped this would be a convenient excuse to sidestep the role of a sovereign to which God was calling him.

But Samuel, the venerable prophet, was persistent. He was determined to prepare the young man towering above him for the task of leading his obdurate nation. Brushing aside all of Saul's objections he took him and his servant into the midst of the gathering of local people and placed him in the most honored place at the banquet table.

With a stroke of enormous significance to all assembled, Samuel commanded that the choicest cut of the shoulder portion be set before Saul. At once everyone assembled knew the powerful import of this action. This shoulder roast was the special heave offering of sacrifice restricted for and dedicated to the lofty service of the priesthood. It was the portion that denoted the rôle of those chosen of God to guide his people in spiritual matters (read carefully Exodus 29:22–28).

In profound symbolical language Samuel was conveying to Saul the intent that as a chosen king he was responsible to rule Israel in a spiritual dimension. It was not enough that Israel's leaders be merely judicial monarchs. They were also required to be spiritual shepherds, so to speak.

To emphasize this aspect Samuel addressed the somewhat shaken young stalwart with this stern command: *"Behold that which is left! Set it before thee, and eat; for unto this time hath it been kept for thee . . ."* (1 Samuel 9:24).

So in solemn, lofty ritual, the handsome young man from an obscure little family in Benjamin partook of a priestly feast with the most honored prophet in Israel. It was a moving event . . . a special moment!

Its spiritual significance far outweighed its symbolism. For in truth the great seer of the Most High had skillfully brought Saul to a great divide in his walk with God. In two swift, stabbing statements he had placed before the determined young man a lifelong choice.

The first, *"Set not your mind on the asses—they are found,"* (v. 20) was a challenge to turn from his old interests, his preoccupation with personal possessions, his familiar pursuits.

The second, *"Set before you the sacrifice of service and the spiritual interests of eternal worth!"* (see 1 Samuel 10:8) was a call to divine duties.

Saul stood now challenged in spirit to either serve himself or to serve the Lord as a special servant king. It was a poignant point in his career. Later events clearly indicated that he opted to serve himself.

For, when eventually he returned home after being with Samuel, the first to meet him was his uncle. On inquiring what had transpired Saul reported only that he had searched for the donkeys which Samuel assured him had been found. Obviously asses still occupied prior place in the young man's interests. He had a mindset for the beasts. Eventually he would make an absolute ass of himself because of this refusal to re-focus his affection on the things of God.

Even on the crowning occasion when Samuel was to set him before Israel as their demanded monarch, Saul could not be found. Finally he was discovered hiding himself amongst the saddles and gear of his beloved beasts. In his calamitous choice of donkeys above divine rulership over Israel, Saul at the outset of his reign had ruled against the government of God. He was determined to have his own way . . . to do his own thing . . . to serve himself.

We who look askance at this tragic series of events may marvel that a man could be so stubborn. Who would settle for being a donkey driver when he could be a monarch of the Most High?

Yet each of us is faced, at some point in life, with a similar choice. The Spirit of the Almighty calls each of us away from our self-centered preoccupations to serve as priests and kings to our God (Revelation 5:9–10).

But sorrow upon sorrow, both to ourselves, to Christ and to others, like Saul, most of us prefer to do our own thing in life, to please ourselves rather than our Lord.

2
Saul's Preparation for Kingship

When Israel demanded a king from God, Samuel knew full well the nation was putting itself in serious jeopardy. But when the man chosen was Saul from Gibeah, the prophet's spiritual concern was even more acute. The town of Gibeah in the tiny tribe of Benjamin bore a dreadful stigma in the history of Israel.

Saul had been painfully honest when he showed amazement that anyone from his tribe and his ill-reputed community would be selected as the first monarch. He had every reason to be aghast.

Gibeah is the town where the man from Ephraim, unnamed in Scripture, stopped overnight with his young concubine from Bethlehem. They were invited into an old man's home as strangers. Later some local ruffians, a band of homosexuals, beat on the door demanding the visitor be brought out so they could engage in sexual perversion with him.

Instead of submitting to these vile demands the visitor pushed his beautiful young concubine out the door into the darkness. Like a pack of ravening predators the perverts rushed upon the poor girl, raping and abusing her in animal acts until dawn. At break of day she lay dead upon the doorstep, a victim of their brutal behavior.

In outrage the man from Ephraim bore her mangled, bloody body home. He dismembered it in twelve pieces. Each of the twelve terrible portions was sent to a tribe in Israel, with a note demanding whether such appalling deeds should be permitted among the people. The action galvanized the entire nation into action. Israel's men of war went into repeated battle against Benjamin until the final death toll was some 40,000 Israelis fallen, and no fewer than 25,100 Benjaminites.

So drastic was the destruction that eventually only a tiny handful of several hundred men survived in Benjamin. It was virtual genocide for Israel. But it revealed boldly the terrible consequences of sexual aberrations in a human society (read Judges 19–21).

Those of the twentieth century who are inclined to dismiss lightly the increasing influence of the gay community need to reflect on this event. It reveals the awesome peril in which a sexually perverted people stands before God.

Because of such a background Samuel took it upon himself to interest young Saul in spiritual matters. The next dawn, after the day in which the two had shared the feast of the heave offering, Samuel would send him on his way home.

But before that the prophet took the youth to the top of his house and there in the privacy of the sun deck shared spiritual truth with him. For hours Samuel gave the towering giant complete details of what his duties would be both before God and man. After all, Saul was to be his successor. Samuel was the last of the long retinue of judges in Israel. He had years and years of experience in leading this obdurate nation. It was the sum total of all his wisdom, knowledge and spiritual insights which he passed on to Saul that memorable day.

Saul knew full well that no mortal man, in his own human limitations, could lead a difficult nation like Israel aright. He would need the supernatural guidance of the Almighty. He would need divine direction from God's gracious Spirit. He would need a special endowment for spiritual as well as judicial service to his people.

Saul was not, to this point, a man suited to such lofty duties. A magnificent physique, a handsome appearance, perhaps charisma of personality—even a strong and determined will—are not sufficient credentials to be chosen as a leader.

There must be the sterling qualities of spiritual understanding, a sensitivity to the guidance of God's Spirit, a profound respect for the lofty laws of God—a deep desire above all else to do His will. As Joshua had demonstrated so brilliantly 300 years before, it was implicit faith in God and immediate compliance with His commands that guaranteed good government and startling success for a nation.

It remained to be seen if Saul could do the same.

At dawn the next day Samuel emphasized again the enormous importance for Saul to hear and respond positively to the Word of God. God's law should be the law of his life.

Samuel then led Saul outside the town to send him on his way. Before parting the prophet drew a small vial of oil from the folds of his robe. In solemn obedience to the command of God he anointed Saul to be king over his people. Then he bestowed on him a kiss of honor and respect.

Samuel advised the young monarch that as he traveled

home to Gibeah several significant events would occur. First he would meet two men who would clearly confirm to him that his father's asses had been found—that now his father was searching for him.

Secondly he would meet other strangers bearing kids, bread and wine (see 1 Samuel 10:3). They would share their bread with him. This was significant since when he came to Samuel he had no bread at all to bestow upon the prophet.

The bread was indicative of much more than merely barley loaves. It spoke profoundly of spiritual truth and a clear comprehension of God's commands. In this area Saul was truly destitute as later events in his life would demonstrate. He needed spiritual bread as surely as he now was given temporal bread to share with others.

Most significant, on his way home he would meet a band of young prophets, praising and making music to the Lord. In their company the Spirit of the Lord God would come upon him and he too would prophesy.

Samuel looked at the handsome king standing so tall and straight before him. With piercing gaze and quiet voice he made the heart-stirring pronouncement: *"You will be turned (changed) into another man"* (see 1 Samuel 10:6).

The wise old seer knew, and God's Spirit knew that it would take the very life of the living Lord active in this young donkey driver to make him fit for royal service to his people. There simply had to be a profound change in his character if he was to be a mighty monarch amongst men.

All his life, Samuel had served Israel as a noble judge. He had a remarkable record of fine achievements before both God and men. The secret of his success had always been his implicit submission to the guidance of God's

Spirit coupled with prompt obedience to the Word of God.

What had been true for him had likewise been true for Israel's chosen leaders of outstanding merit. Men like Moses, Joshua and Gideon were great, not in their own might or skill, but in their total allegiance to Jehovah God. They were magnificent in their day because of their willingness to do God's will at any cost. They were totally expendable for the Lord.

So now Samuel pressed upon Saul the absolute imperative of doing whatever God commanded. *"God is with you!"* The prophet assured him. *"God is here! God is present! Simply carry out his commands!"* (see 1 Samuel 10:7).

It was a declaration of enormous importance.

The very first test of whether or not Saul took this charge seriously would be seven days later when the two men would meet again at Gilgal. The prophet's direct word to him was that he was to wait there for his arrival.

Saul took leave of Samuel. Almost instantaneously the Spirit of God moved upon him as foretold. He was endued with the ability to prophesy. This special capacity was not only to speak of the future but also to clearly converse of God's purposes for His people.

The sudden transformation attracted immediate public attention. Those who knew Saul well could scarcely believe the change that had come over him. In astonishment they asked, *"Is Saul also amongst the prophets?"* (see v. 11). They could scarcely credit the fact that a man like Kish, whose name means "a snare," could produce a son of such spiritual stature. In fact, the entire episode became a byword in the region. With startling speed the word of Saul's metamorphosis sped across the country.

On the surface, at least, it would seem that Israel would

be blessed not only with a handsome monarch in physical majesty, but also honored with a royal king of profound spiritual power. All the outward signs seemed so reassuring. Surely Saul would become a national hero.

The first inkling that Israel's initial choice of a king was faulty came almost immediately. For when Saul encountered his uncle, the first of his family to meet him after being absent so long, he was asked a very simple question, *"Where did you go?"* (see v. 14).

Saul's abrupt and off-hand reply that he and his servant had merely gone in search of the missing asses, and sought Samuel's aid in locating them, was a clear signal that his priorities were in total disarray. Asses still occupied first place in his thinking. His soul was set on donkeys.

He mentioned not a word of all the profound and mighty spiritual issues Samuel had discussed with him in such moving conversations. The things of God, it seems, carried little or no weight with the tough-willed young worldling. The spiritual transformations were not worth mentioning.

Ultimately this selfish, self-centered mindset would be Saul's total undoing. It would bring him to utter ruin. It would spell his eventual rejection by God as king. It would demand that a replacement be found in David as one fit to fill the role of a royal sovereign over Israel.

We who read the record of Saul's response to God, may, if we are spiritually perceptive, see reflected in his conduct our own characters. We are startled to see in his intransigence our own behavior mirrored clearly.

Many of us who claim boldly to be "born again," to be filled with God's Spirit, to be new creatures in Christ, still do not have our priorities in proper order.

Too often, far too often, our asses, our pursuits, our passions, our pleasures, our possessions are much more important to us than anything God ever did in our lives!

3

Israel Receives a King

Under the intimate direction of Jehovah God, Samuel had decided that the day had come when Israel as a nation should receive her first monarch. As intimated earlier, this was not God's highest or best intention for this difficult people. Rather it was their own insistent demand to which He acceded.

The grizzled old prophet, gray and stooped after long years of service to his people, summoned them all to assemble at Mizpeh. An electric sort of excitement crackled through the massed crowd. Who would be chosen as their new sovereign? From which tribe, community and family would he emerge? A brand new dynasty was being established in Israel. What sort of person would be selected?

Solemnly, in great thundering statements, Samuel again reminded his compatriots of the serious step they were taking. Speaking on behalf of the Most High God he reasserted: *"I delivered you from all of your oppressors. Yet this day you have rejected your God who saved you out of all tribulations. You have demanded to have a king set over you!"* (see 1 Samuel 10:18–19).

The drastic decision was theirs.

What they insisted upon they would receive!

They would have human royalty rather than heavenly royalty.

They would have to endure the awful consequences.

Tribe by tribe, clan by clan, in their assembled thousands, each integral group of people was ordered to present itself in honor before God. This was a ritual of submission to the supreme sovereignty of Jehovah. Samuel the high priest was here enacting his final great role in spiritual authority over Israel.

Using the divine unction of *Urim and Thummim* for supernatural guidance, he meticulously inspected each tribe and clan as they stood at attention before him. The choice fell upon the little band from Benjamin. Then in turn the family clan of Matri and Kish was selected. And from them Saul was drawn by name.

It was an orderly, accepted process familiar to this strange people. Joshua had used this method to determine long ago that Achan had disobeyed God and brought terrible defeat on Israel at the battle of Ai. It was the method used by Joshua under the high priest Eleazer to divide and apportion all of Palestine to the nation of Israel.

On this momentous day in Israel's tragic history it was the ordained way in which Saul was chosen as a king in the presence of all his people. Only one thing was awry—Saul himself could not be found. He had gone into hiding.

Perhaps the very prospect of ruling such a perverse people overwhelmed the young giant. Or it was his own personal reluctance to serve others that made him hide. Perhaps his penchant for donkeys and livestock was an all-consuming passion.

For, when at last he was discovered, by means of guidance from God, Saul was found buried beneath the saddle blankets, panniers and usual array of baggage borne by the sturdy little beasts. It was an absurd act. If it had not been so sad, it might well have been ludicrous and laughable.

There Saul stood, towering well over six feet, head and shoulders above the massed crowd crushing in all around him. No doubt strands of straw and wisps of hay clung to his clothes and stuck in his handsome head of hair. Dust and dirt soiled his robes. He had just been rolled out from beneath the smelly, sweat-stained saddle blankets of his beloved donkeys. He looked like anything but a monarch!

Without apology or delay Samuel simply stood the young giant up before all the nation and stated, *"See the one whom God has chosen. There is no other like him amongst the people!"* (see v. 24).

In a roaring thunder of mounting applause all the crowd shouted in unison, *"God save the king!"* How little they realized in this moment of emotion that it was they who would need to be saved from the tyranny of such a disastrous ruler.

We are not told this, but without doubt in that massed multitude stood a man named Jesse, a sturdy sheep man from Judah. Looking at Saul he must have mused to himself, *"What an honor to be a father like Kish, to be a king in Israel."* Little did he dream that one day his own son, David, would be chosen of God to supplant the magnificent man now standing as monarch over Israel. Time changed many things.

The people dispersed quickly from Mizpeh, returning to their homes, towns and rural hamlets. All would be well now for Israel. She had her king. No need to be concerned about invasions or conquest by enemy invaders. Saul would save the nation.

Unhappily for Saul, not everyone in Israel adored him.

A certain group of young stalwarts whose spirits God had touched, turning their wills to serve him, had gathered their forces around Saul. But by the same measure, there were those who despised his kingship, doubting if indeed he could deliver Israel in its hour of danger.

It was a difficult position for the young monarch. Happily he was wise enough to ignore the insults. In a short time his power in battle would become known to the nation. His actions would speak louder than any words he might utter in self-defense.

There are those who assert that Saul's behavior at the beginning of his reign indicated a man humble in spirit, self-effacing and contrite in heart. In part this may have been true. But from the perspective of later events— especially his attitude and actions against Jonathan, his own son, David, who was to succeed him, and others— it is apparent Saul was already showing the early signs of a decided schizophrenia.

Just at this juncture in the history of Israel, the Ammonites, an offshoot of the nation originating with Lot's youngest daughter, threatened to invade Jabesh-Gilead across the Jordan. Not only did they wish to enslave them, but, even much more deplorable, they intended to bore out their right eyes as an insult to Israel.

The elders of Jabesh begged for a week's reprieve. They would seek help from Israel. If none was forthcoming they would submit to the invaders, suffering their awful cruelty.

It was natural that their plight be made known first to Saul's little town of Gibeah. Jabesh hoped he would come to their rescue. But beyond this there were the ancient intimate ties between Jabesh and Benjamin. When Israel annihilated all the men and women of Benjamin except a few hundred warriors, they had gone to

Jabesh-Gilead to procure young virgin brides for the few warriors. So Saul's own lineage traced back to Jabesh.

The news of the impending invasion threw Gibeah into a panic. The villagers burst into tears. It seemed all was lost. But it was not. God had his man of the hour in Gibeah, reprehensible as its past record may have been.

Saul came home that evening driving his beloved donkeys from their range. He found the community in an uproar of anguish and inquired for the cause of the commotion and weeping. The news enraged him.

The Spirit of God, given to him in such plenitude for service, now stirred him deeply. In a bold action—vividly reminiscent of the man from Ephraim whose concubine had been cut into pieces and sent to each tribe in Israel—Saul now slaughtered a pair of his own oxen. Severing them into small pieces he sent portions of the bloody flesh to every tribe in the nation.

A solemn warning accompanied the grisly messages. *"Come out to battle for Saul and Samuel or your own oxen will be slaughtered in this way"* (see 1 Samuel 11:8).

It was the first royal edict issued by Israel's fledgling monarch. To a man the entire nation responded, most of them awed by Saul's bold action. In a matter of hours a force of nearly a third of a million men was mustered for war. Some 300,000 came from the tribes of Israel, and 30,000 from Judah.

Saul, with enormous self-confidence, sent word back to Jabesh-Gilead that aid would come to them by noon the next day. Elated, the messengers raced home with the news.

With remarkable skill and speed Saul divided his huge army into three divisions. Immediately they were dispatched against the Ammonites. All this was achieved under cover of darkness. The Israelis went into action during the dawn of the morning watch (2–6 A.M.), taking the enemy by surprise. The rout was so complete and the victory so overwhelming that by noon the invaders were scattered as dust before the wind.

It was a tremendous triumph for Saul. Those loyal to him from the outset now demanded the death of those who had deprecated his kingship. But Saul was in an expansive mood, making no move to wreak vengeance on his detractors.

Instead, in a rare and generous outburst of gratitude to God, he shouted, *"Today the Lord has saved Israel"* (see 1 Samuel 11:13). This was perhaps the most noble thing Saul ever did in all his life. It seemed like such an auspicious omen of great hope for Israel's future.

Caught up in the excitement of the great victory, Samuel decided on the spot it would be in order for Israel to celebrate with a second coronation of her new king. He could hardly be blamed for this. After all, the first occasion at Mizpeh had been such a dreadful debacle.

At Samuel's urging all of Israel again gathered in a huge assembly at Gilgal. Gilgal means, "Where the reproach is removed." Surely again the shaky, stumbling start of Israel's sovereignty as a new nation was now behind them. Their magnificent monarch had established his credentials as a legitimate leader. Now was the hour to celebrate the exhilarating occasion with singing, dancing and suitable sacrifices of peace and praise to the Most High.

This is probably the only case in human history when a would-be king received the dubious honor of a double coronation. But Saul was a double-minded man whose character demanded much from others.

4

Receiving Heaven's Royalty

In very truth, and in actual fact, Israel now had received her own chosen human royalty. Saul was firmly established as monarch in the realm. A new line of kings had come in to govern the nation. In essence the kingdom of God's own chosen people had been torn from His own great hands and given over to the fickle fortunes of human hands.

In a word, Israel had rejected heaven's royalty and chosen a mere man as monarch instead.

It was a disastrous decision of tremendous peril. And, but for the generous mercy of the Lord God Himself, it would have spelled the nation's total destruction. Actually, in due course this did occur, when Israel was overcome by her oppressors, taken back into bondage, then eventually scattered like barley chaff to the four winds of the world.

The importance of this choice cannot be narrated in a book of this kind only as an ominous historical event. For it is much more than that. It is a profound spiritual principle that engages every person who comes into contact with the Living Lord. It is the most crucial issue, by far, that faces any individual who enters the family of God . . . who comes to Christ . . . who by His Spirit is made aware of the sovereignty of the Almighty.

Our Lord when He was here spoke more about *"the kingdom of God"* than any other subject. It was foremost in His attention. Is it in ours? Do we understand it? What does it mean "to receive Christ as heaven's royalty"?

In recent human history there has been a general world-wide revolt against monarchies. In North America, for instance, the so-called American Revolution against King George III of Britain, and the less drastic action of Canada in repatriating its own constitution, are examples of our break with the restraints of royalty.

In the minds of many, through the teaching of history, the rule of a king has been equated with that which was tyrannical and aggressive. Subconsciously many associate royalty with repression. Therefore it is not surprising that people in contemporary society tend to reject the concept of coming under control of a king.

Quite the opposite! We often pride ourselves upon our democratic ideals. We rejoice in our freedoms, even though often abused and misused for selfish ends. We insist all men should be free to determine their destiny in any way they choose.

The result is that in truth many of us are caught up in a conflict of ideas within. On the one hand our secular education convinces us that royalty and the rule of a sovereign are something archaic. Yet, on the other hand, the teaching of Scripture is that the only true spiritual freedom available to a soul is to come under the control of Christ, the King of Glory, the Prince of Peace, the Sovereign of the Universe.

The single truth is that just as Israel rejected the Royalty of the Most High in selecting Saul's rule, so do we today in our private lives.

So the hard and searching questions must be asked. "Is God, in Christ, entitled to rule over the human race? Does the Lord really have the credentials to command our loyal allegiance? Is He truly Sovereign of our universe?"

If we look to human philosophy and man's politics for the answers, the reply would be a resounding *"No!"* For the inherent pride of the human will is to declare with incredible vehemence, *"I am king in my own castle!"*

Yet, the amazing declaration of God's Word to us as a human race is that He, and He alone, is our rightful royalty. The special revelation of the Scriptures is the remarkable disclosure that our God has certain inalienable claims upon us as His people, as His citizens, as His loyal, loving servants.

These are based upon three major propositions, which in the main are rejected by human philosophy and scorned by science. Because these propositions are despised by modern thought many in the church try to come to some sort of comfortable accommodation with respect to the ultimate rule of heaven's royalty within their lives. They seek simply to shunt the idea to the side.

If we are to enter the kingdom of God—if we are to become children of the Most High—that cannot be done.

Here are the three foundational facts which underlie Christ's legitimate claims upon us as a benevolent monarch.

1) He is the One who made us. It is He who in the grandeur of His own designs in the eternal realm first conceived of a human race with a capacity to know Him, to commune with Him, to love Him, to enjoy Him.

Not only did He desire to have a race of humans upon whom He could lavish His love, but He also wanted them to bring profound pleasure to Him by their response to His overtures of compassion and care.

He, the Creator of the universe, arranged for planet earth to be prepared as a suitable environment and habitat for human beings. With its sun and moon and stars, it was to be a stimulating setting of enormous benefit to man's body and incredible inspiration to man's soul: A sphere wherein the Spirit of the living God could move in majesty upon the spirit of man.

But many of our scientists, psychologists and educators, our so-called "thinkers," reject all the above. They insist human beings are but the ultimate end product of the blind evolutionary process. They contend we came into being by pure chance. They assert man is only a dual being with body and mind (person). They claim the realm of the spirit is but a figment of fantasy.

Still the irrefutable fact remains that deep down in his innermost instincts man, if he is utterly honest, realizes he is far too remarkable a creature to have appeared without a Creator. It is beyond all the bounds of probability.

Our profound yearnings of spirit to know God; our eternal quest for truth; our longings for hope beyond death; our ceaseless search for rest and peace which comes only from Him attest to the fact He made us for Himself.

So His claim upon us as Supreme Creator is unshakable.

2) The second tremendous revelation given to us by God Himself is that He sustains the entire universe by the energy of His own person. He controls the cosmos. He and He alone maintains the meticulous laws, principles and power that govern the earth as well as all of outer space.

Were it not for Him at work everywhere, the result would be horrendous chaos, not only in the heavens but also in the biota. Everywhere we turn to search for new knowledge we are astonished at the order, the harmony, the deliberate designs, the incredible intricacy that govern the realms of physics, chemistry, biology, botany or a hundred other disciplines.

In other words, we live in a realm of remarkable law and order. It is established in profound wisdom and love. We are the recipients of remarkable benefits we did not design. We are supported and sustained by an environment beautiful in conception, magnificent in its capacity to sustain us as people, together with all the other multitudes of life forms upon the planet.

In short, it may be said in all truth: *"In him we live, and move, and have our being"* (Acts 17:28).

David, the Shepherd King, who was to succeed Saul, wrote scores of poems and psalms to attest to this fact. He, more than Saul ever knew, recognized the royal might and majesty of the living Lord in the universe.

And it is appropriate to state here that it was David's willingness to submit to the supremacy of God's Spirit that insured him a greatness surpassing anything Saul would ever experience.

3) The third great self-disclosure given to us mortals by God is that He has a legitimate claim upon us in a spiritual dimension. All of us in ignorance, folly and incredible pride tend to stray from Him. We prefer to go our own way in powerful choices of perverse self-assertion. Our surging self-will, as with Israel of old, prefers to reject the government of God. We do not want to be subject to His sovereignty, even though He is so benevolent and has only our own best interests in mind.

The consequence has meant never-ending suffering for Him and never-ending pain for us. It is He who has taken the tremendous steps necessary to deliver us from our dilemma. Out of our despair He brings us into hope. Out of our spiritual death He brings us into life. Out of our dreadful darkness He brings us into the light of His own wondrous presence.

This is the great good news of His coming to us. It is the stirring salvation given to us so generously through His perfect life, His gracious death and His thrilling resurrection.

He is the One who redeems us. He restores us, if we will let Him, to Himself. He heals the breach between us. He claims us as His own children.

He who is heaven's royalty has done all that is necessary to free us from slavery to sin, servitude to Satan, submission to the terrible tyranny of our own selfishness.

He offers us total freedom to become His loyal, loving subjects.

The formidable question which all of us here face is this, *"As heaven's royalty will I receive Him as King?"* Unfortunately most do not.

The reason is twofold. First, many are taught that to receive Christ is the same as receiving a gift. One just reaches out to take and possess it. Not so with a royal monarch! To receive a royal personage implies exactly the opposite. It means the recipient presents himself to the monarch to be owned and possessed by royalty. It is to declare one's total devotion and loyalty to his sovereign.

Few of us ever submit ourselves in this way to the gracious government of God. We will not submit to the sovereignty of His Spirit. We will not come under the benevolent control of the living Lord Jesus Christ, King of heaven and earth.

The second reason for this is the steel-like resistance

40

of our wills to His. We refuse to capitulate to His claims upon us. We insist on being little kings in our own castles! We are determined to make our own decisions and so seal our destiny, even if it means our ultimate destruction.

This is what Israel did as a nation. It was the same path Saul chose as a self-willed monarch who came to a dreadful demise, as we shall see.

But the eternal generous offer extended to each of us is: *"He came unto his own, and his own received him not. But as many as received him, to them gave he the power to become the sons of God . . ."* (John 1:11–12).

5

Saul's Shaky Start

It was this powerful tendency, inherent in men, to take command of their own affairs, that troubled the prophet Samuel so deeply. He was retiring now from the responsibility of ruling Israel as their last judge. He was transferring his leadership to the new and untried king.

With the whole nation assembled before him the old, gray-headed stalwart challenged the people to consider the crucial choice they had made. With his own profound spiritual wisdom he knew full well the future for Israel was fraught with peril. Instead of being guided by God, they had submitted their lives to the fickle hands of a mere man. With blazing eyes Samuel stood before his compatriots and in thundering tones rehearsed his own history to them. He had walked before them in total integrity since his early childhood. Since that still, dark night, when as a small lad he responded to the clarion call of the Almighty by saying, *"Speak, Lord, for thy servant heareth"* (1 Samuel 3:9, 10), he had never once defrauded any man or woman.

In a society and culture where bribery and corruption

were the common way of life, Samuel had not once acted unjustly. His record was impeccable. What a tremendous tribute to his fine character! It was the strength of his devotion to the Lord that had delivered Israel from the oppression of her enemies.

This was noble leadership of the highest order. And Samuel reminded the nation again that it was this spiritual rule of law and order under God's great hand that they were repudiating.

Casting his burning gaze over the massed multitude he reminded them, too, of Jehovah's great faithfulness to them since the day of their deliverance from Egypt. Yet, they, in response, had turned away from Him to pursue the false gods and strange beliefs of the pagan nations around them.

He warned them in ominous terms that the new regime on which they were embarking under a mortal king could spell dreadful danger. Their only hope of survival as a people was to receive the Lord God, to serve Him faithfully and obey His commands without further rebellion against His rule.

The beloved and stooped old seer was not at all sure Israel could or would do this. He had lived too long and knew too well how perverse and proud his people were. His wide experience as a judge for so many years gave him grounds to doubt whether Israel could possibly survive under Saul.

Almost in tears, deeply moved by the peril facing his people, the ancient prophet begged Israel to be loyal to the Lord. This was his final farewell, so to speak. He felt constrained to cry out a last warning to his wayward associates. To love God was to obey Him. To rebel against Him was to court utter ruin.

It was a solemn note of warning that has not lost its

force across the ensuing centuries. The same clarion call comes to our contemporary society of the twentieth century. *"Serve the Lord God and live. Turn from him and perish."* The choice is ours!

To confirm the credibility of his challenge to Israel, Samuel then called for a deluge of rain and rumbling thunderstorms to sweep over the country. Though it was late summer, the season of harvest, hot and dry, the sky suddenly darkened. Great black clouds rolled in across the hills and a gigantic cloudburst drenched the dry ground.

It was an awesome spectacle, a startling phenomenon. The people in fear and panic knew that they had heard from the Almighty. He had endorsed the message delivered by His servant.

Samuel, with his ancient affection for his stiff-necked nation, again urged them to follow the Lord. Then in touching tenderness he assured them, like a loving father, that he would not cease to pray for them. He knew that in his retirement there was no other single service of greater import that he could render to both God and man.

Not only would he pray for Israel, but he would also persevere in trying to teach them the proper and righteous way to walk with God. His twilight years would not be wasted in self-indulgence. Instead they would be spent in lively service to his generation.

What was true for Samuel is no less true for us. In our North American society there is a large number of elderly people—many of them Christians. They, too, can devote their time and energy to no greater good than to spread themselves in intercession to God for others. To fail to do this, as Samuel declared so vehemently on this occasion, is to grieve God Himself. It is also to betray others around us who may not know the good and right way to follow Christ.

I am a senior citizen myself. God's gracious Spirit has laid upon my spirit three special concerns to pray for continuously: 1) The leadership of His church worldwide. That godly men of truth, loyal to His Word, would arise boldly to strengthen His body of believers. 2) A definite spiritual awakening amongst those engaged in the media, so that many who promulgate worldly philosophies and false ideologies will come to know Christ, the Truth. 3) Leaders of government at all levels, to the end that those of integrity and credibility will be brought to office in all nations.

It was fortunate indeed for Saul that a righteous servant of the Most High was behind the scenes interceding on his behalf. Israel's military forces were in utter disarray. Apparently most of the people lived almost as hostages to the Philistines, their ancient enemy. The record given to us of this period emphasizes that only Saul and Jonathan were fully armed (1 Samuel 13:22). Perhaps partly for this reason Saul had been chosen as king.

It seems incongruous that at this stage of her dismal history Israel did not even have artisans skilled in the smelting and shaping of iron. There were not even primitive blacksmiths who could forge weapons or fashion farm tools. Many Israelis had to resort to Philistine craftsmen to sharpen their plowshares, axes and mattocks.

It was a deplorable sort of dependency on one's arch enemy. Little wonder that only the restraining hand of the Almighty had preserved the nation from utter annihilation up to this point.

Saul, in an unsteady first step, decided to recruit about one percent of the would-be warriors available to him. He elected to establish a unit of about 2,000 men under his command and half that number under young Jonathan, his son. It was rather a pitiful start when we recall that nearly one third of a million men had risen to the defense of Jabesh-Gilead.

Anyway, his young blood eager for battle, Jonathan made a surprise attack and killed a small garrison of the Philistines at Geba. It was an aggressive action. Immediately the enemy mustered their formidable forces for war against Israel—amongst them some 30,000 battle chariots as well as over 6,000 mounted cavalrymen.

The outlook for Israel was ominous. As of old, in the days of Gideon, Saul's people panicked. They fled into the forests, caves and rocky hideouts for refuge.

The handful of men chosen to accompany Saul felt unsure of themselves. Perhaps they would be the first to come under attack. In fear and trembling they, too, began to lose heart, turned tail, and fled, abandoning their new king.

Saul could see his position was precarious. His people were in mortal peril. Only about 600 warriors now stood true to him. Where could he turn for help?

In his extremity the inexperienced, stumbling, new monarch decided to turn to the veteran Samuel. After all, as judge over the nation Saul had preserved Israel all his life from invasion from the Philistines. Perhaps the aged prophet, with help from Jehovah, could pull it off again.

Saul set off for Gilgal. It was there he had been instructed to meet Samuel before. But in his arrogance he had failed to do so. Now in utter disarray he decided he should go. It would mean waiting a week for Samuel to show up. Who knew what might happen in the meantime?

The days dragged by with mounting apprehension on

the part of Saul. More of his men were deserting. The Philistine forces were on the march. Three enemy divisions were surging into Israel on a rampage as armed raiders.

Unable to restrain himself any longer, Saul decided he would not wait for the prophet to come and offer a sacrifice on his behalf. Instead, taking the bull by the horns, he ordered a sacrifice prepared which he himself offered up.

It was a precipitous action of direct disobedience. Just at that juncture Samuel showed up! He was beside himself with astonishment at the king's folly. What a drastic act! He had flown in the face of all the divine direction given to him by God.

In the heat of the moment and the excitement of their encounter, Saul did not seem to realize the horrendous consequences of his deliberate disregard for the Word of the Lord. From this terrible moment it was destined that the royal monarchy would be torn from his grasp. God Himself would select a substitute sovereign to reign in his stead. And that royal ruler would be a young shepherd lad from the rugged hills of Judeah—*David* by name.

What Saul had demonstrated at Gilgal was a stubborn, impetuous, strong self-will that insisted on asserting itself. He was obviously not suited to serve under the sovereignty of God. Again and again this trait would lead to his downfall. He was a man incapable of coming under divine control.

The principle is an all-important one for each of us. Will we wait patiently and comply with Christ's wishes? Or must we push ahead with our own ideas and insist on using our own initiative? Are we the ones who will "call the shots," or are we ready to respond in hearty good will to what heaven's royalty arranges for us?

To have our own way is to end up in disarray.

To quietly do our Father's will is to know strength and security!

6

Jonathan Storms the Enemy Stronghold

The stern rebuke from Samuel, instead of bringing a sense of profound remorse to Saul, seemed instead to plunge him into a state of pathetic reaction. Had he been a man sensitive in spirit to God's purposes he would have repented of his wrong, sought reconciliation, then gone out to attack the Philistine invaders.

Instead he chose to idle away his time sitting in the pleasant shade of a leafy pomegranate tree in his home village of Gibeah. Like the olive, the pomegranate, from ancient times, spoke of peace and well-being. It was a symbol of repose. Pomegranate wine was strong drink surpassing any made from grapes. It dulled the senses and unbalanced the mind.

Saul's odd behavior spoke of "peace, peace," when in reality the Philistine forces already stood threatening Israel with utter annihilation. One advance garrison had already established a formidable stronghold in the rocky heights of Michmash.

Jonathan, Saul's son, now considered as the first prince in Israel, was not prepared to sit in idle contemplation of the enemy threat. Alone, except for the company of his brave young armorbearer, he decided to test the enemy positions.

Quietly Jonathan slipped away. No one even knew he had left on such a dangerous mission. It was typical of the remarkable youth. He was not a showman.

He was a heroic young Israeli who had great confidence in God Himself. He was cut from the same cloth as men like Moses, Joshua, Caleb and Gideon. His implicit conviction was that no matter how overwhelming the odds were against him, *"One man with God was a winner."* It was the Almighty who could enable him to overcome the enemy.

Jonathan was not looking for a spectacular sort of miracle with which to impress his associates. Nor was he engaging in a foolhardy act of bravado. He was moving quietly, seeking God's guidance, anxious to have Jehovah reveal His power to His people.

It was not Jonathan's ambition to become a rising star in Israel's new royal family. His one aim was to give God a chance to prove again that He could save Israel either by many or by few. His burning inner hope was that he might in fact become a shining spear in the hand of the Most High.

As the two men approached the enemy-held territory the young armorbearer assured Jonathan of his total allegiance. He would not desert his daring master. Like Gideon's brave servant who accompanied him into the camp of the Midianites, here was a stalwart ready to risk his life for his commander.

Jonathan was not rash or impulsive. He was not one to rush ahead of God. He explained to his armorbearer carefully each step he took. He would reveal himself to the Philistines in their rocky hideout.

If the enemy were to threaten to come down to the low ground, they would stand firm awaiting the attack. If, on the other hand, they challenged Jonathan to climb the ridge for combat, they would go up, sure of triumph under God's mighty hand.

As soon as they spotted Jonathan, the bold invaders taunted him: *"Look, the Hebrews are crawling out of their holes. Come on up, we will show you a thing or two!"* (see 1 Samuel 14:11).

It was enough!

This was the clear, ringing challenge to join battle on the rock ridges. No matter how formidable and dangerous the ascent they would climb the rock outcrops on hands and knees to get to the invaders.

Jonathan and his companion had no audience of supporting onlookers to cheer for them. They were not putting on some dazzling performance to impress their associates. This was not a bit of youthful folly.

It was a man moving quietly in great strength and with enormous confidence in God. It was a man unafraid to risk his life in the hands of the Lord. It was Jehovah, not Jonathan, who this day would again demonstrate His deliverance of Israel.

But Jonathan was the catalyst that precipitated the action. It was his faith that moved the might and majesty of God. Sweating and scrambling up the great rock outcrop, he put himself in great peril for his people.

This is faith in action. Faith is more than mere belief. Faith demands a positive response from a person's will to the point that he will act on the authority of God's Word to him. Such people see beyond the obstacles of the moment to the great achievements God can bring to reality in any situation, no matter how formidable the odds appear.

As Jonathan and his comrade climbed the rocks in full view of the Philistines it may have seemed utter insanity to the enemy. How easy to wipe out two warriors on their way up! How simple to slaughter the two adventurers climbing toward them! The whole thing was nothing more than a mere diversion that would inject a bit of excitement into the hot day. Soon hot, dark, human blood would stain the rocks. Soon sharp-eyed vultures would wheel in the sky waiting for their gory banquet of human flesh. Soon a swarm of flies would buzz over the dead carcasses of the fallen.

But strange as it seemed, the slain would not be the two young Israelis—but rather the host of the Philistine hordes who had invaded the land. For, as soon as Jonathan scaled the steep ridge, he charged into hand-to-hand combat with the enemy.

It was a ferocious encounter. Few details are given of the incredible combat. We are simply told that in short order about twenty Philistine warriors lay dead on the ground, scattered over about half an acre.

The ferocious assault triggered a gigantic earthquake. Not only did the ground, rocks and hills tremble with the shock waves, but so did the emotions of the enemy forces. The violent convulsions of the earth created panic, confusion and blind fear amongst the Philistines.

Again in an action of utter chaos the armed hordes of the enemy began to butcher each other in brutal slaughter. It was almost like a replay of the rout brought upon the Midianites the night Gideon invaded their camp with his three hundred men bearing torches. It was akin to the tremendous victory granted Joshua when huge hailstones rained down upon the Amorites fleeing before his forces.

This was again a tremendous triumph for Israel. It was

being evidenced once more that God the Almighty was their deliverer. It was irrefutable proof that He could put the enemy to flight.

Amid the carnage and confusion Hebrew mercenaries who had been serving the Philistines turned against their erstwhile allies. In open revolt they attacked the invaders and slaughtered the very ones who had armed them for combat against their own countrymen.

The net result was a complete rout of the enemy. What had appeared at dawn that day as a formidable threat to the future of Israel, had simply vanished into oblivion by sundown. It had been a magnificent display of God's might on behalf of His people.

Sitting softly in the cool shade of his green and lovely pomegranate tree, Saul had no idea what was happening in the high country. Sipping on his pomegranate wine, dreaming dreams of peace and plenty, he knew nothing of the furious combat in the hills. Like many moderns he simply assumed that by speaking much of peace, peace would just come drifting sweetly across the country.

Not so! The freedom, survival and destiny of Israel were being forged and secured in the brutal battle raging up on those ridges. Nor did his blurry eyes and dim wits see this until his scouts shouted to him that the Philistines were being routed from their stronghold.

It takes more than pleasant talk, empty rhetoric and skilled diplomacy to bring about peace of any sort in human society. The price for peace is very high. It comes at the cost of personal privation, of total preparedness, of enormous courage and strength in the struggle for survival. The weak are always driven to the wall to be obliterated in cold blood.

In a frenzy of excitement Saul did not even have the presence of mind to order his own men to pursue the

Philistines. Instead he decided to take a roll call to discover who was missing. To his astonishment he found that Jonathan and his armorbearer were gone. He could scarcely credit the fact. Surely his son would not be so rash!

In characteristic double-minded confusion Saul ordered the priest to bring up the ark of God for consultation. Then a few moments later he commanded him to withdraw. What he was to do, how and when, seemed beyond his befuddled brain. He never knew God's will!

Finally in a belated show of strength, the bungling monarch gathered up his armed men and headed for the battle. It was as if it was his feeble effort to add his own loud "hurrah" to the victory cry.

As news of the combat spread across the countryside, timid Israelis climbed out of their caves, emerging from hiding in hills and forests to join in pursuit of the Philistines. It was a remarkable conquest that had been sparked by one man's quiet confidence in the trustworthiness of the Almighty.

As so often happens, it takes one person's courage, initiative and boldness to bring others into action. Saul's indolence might very well have spelled Israel's total defeat at the very beginning of his hopeless reign. Instead, his son's strong faith and brave fortitude in the time of peril enabled God to save His people.

Jonathan was a person who had power with God and man. In loyalty and love for others he was willing to lay down his life, if need be, to save his friends. He was bolder than a lion and swifter than an eagle. He dared danger in order to do God's will.

It was he who would, in later time, become David's dearest friend. They were both forged from the same hard steel, fearless for the Lord.

7

Saul's Foolish Oaths

In characteristic Hebrew fashion, the ancient narrator of the events on this great day of triumph records the personal folly of Saul. He tells of the spiritual mistakes made by Israel's new king. Unlike most modern nations, where there is a distinct cleavage between church and state, in the Hebrew economy their monarch was also expected to be a strong spiritual leader. In a positive way he provided the spiritual standard for those under his dominion.

With a vain show of supposed spiritual zeal Saul ordered his men to fast until sundown. It was sheer stupidity. Sometimes locked in ferocious hand-to-hand combat, his armed warriors (in hot pursuit of the enemy) needed all the support and stamina they could derive from food and drink, wherever they might find it.

Jonathan, of course, being away on his daring escapade with his armorbearer, knew nothing of the curse. While hot on the trail of the fleeing Philistines he came across some honeycombs, dripping with the sweet nectar of the bees. Immediately he paused long enough to enjoy the delicacy that could revive his energy and quicken his weary mind.

The honeycombs were scattered widely at random throughout the wooded terrain. It was a part of the battle rations that primitive men of war often carried into combat. African tribes still do this. The entire comb is consumed: beeswax, grubs, honey and all.

In their terror and consternation at the fearsome earthquake, as well as their own pandemonium, the Philistines in haste jettisoned the honeycombs leaving them as spoils of war for the Israelis. It could have been a tremendous bonus to Saul's men. Instead it was an irksome irritation. For they had become faint and weak with the strenuous combat of the day.

With an intense flash of spiritual perception Jonathan saw the folly of his father's oath: *"My father has troubled the land!"* he shouted in desperation. *"How much greater would have been Israel's conquest today if all the warriors could have eaten freely of the enemy spoils, as I have!"* (see 1 Samuel 14:30).

Jonathan knew full well that because the warriors were weak from exertion and faint from hunger their triumph over the Philistines was less than it might have been. This could have been one of the most memorable victories in Israel's history. It might well have been a day when once for all the Philistines were vanquished as a formidable foe. This should have spelled the end to their never-ending attacks.

Instead, many of the enemy escaped from the Israelis. They were able to return to the sanctuary of their own territory. There they would re-group again to await another opportunity to launch a new invasion of Saul's territory.

When they did return to attack, Saul and all his men

would be intimidated. Only a young shepherd lad would be brave enough to face their might.

The reason for Saul's rash action must be attributed to his intense self-preoccupation. He saw the Philistine invasion as a personal attack on himself. It was, he was sure, an insult to his position as a monarch. With the typical stance of a deranged schizophrenic he felt this was a personal vendetta. He did not have the broad view of a true statesman who saw the peril of his people, much less the honor of God, at stake in the conflict.

Saul wanted only one thing. That was revenge! Not for his nation, but for his own whimsy. He was a man of mixed emotions and miserable moods. All of them fermented in the pit of his own selfish self-interest and stubborn waywardness.

The remarkable aspect of this ominous day was that Saul had sufficient influence with his men that most of them complied with his commands—as absurd as they seemed. But as the day wore on the gnawing hunger and burning thirst under the sweltering sun could not be denied.

First one, then another, like rabid predators leaping on their hopeless prey, the Israelis began to fall on the calves, sheep and oxen left behind by the Philistines. In an orgy of slaughter and wanton butchery they killed the animals, gorging on the raw flesh, drinking the hot salty blood that spurted from the severed veins and arteries.

It is a sight I have seen first hand amongst the Masai of East Africa.

The rapid-fire sequence of events that night are bound to go down in Israel's history as among the most bizarre on record. From the most ancient times, dating as far back as the flood in Noah's time, God had strictly forbidden the eating of animal flesh with blood in it (*see Genesis* 9:4). Again in the precepts of the Levitical law under Moses this principle was proclaimed (*see Leviticus* 17:10–14).

The concept, clearly understood by Israel, was that there was *"life in the blood."* To offer a sacrifice suitable for the propitiation of sin against God it was essential that an innocent animal victim be slain, its spilled blood (poured-out life) being offered as a unique substitute for the offender's new life. All of this looked forward to, and prefigured, the perfect life of God Himself being poured out in the shedding of Christ's blood for lost men at Calvary.

Because of this no one dared to defile himself, much less desecrate the divine ordinance of the Most High, by consuming blood. But Saul's men were tearing the raw flesh with their teeth and slaking their fierce thirst with blood in wild abandon.

Even Saul was outraged and aghast. He saw the enormity of their transgression. In panic he ordered a huge rock to be rolled into view for him. Perhaps he could stand on it to gain the attention of his men. He commanded that every warrior bring his beast before him to be slaughtered in the appropriate way.

Then, for the first time in his life, Saul himself erected an altar to God. It was a case of too little, too late, for in his folly he had failed to seek God's direction in his decisions. Still he felt sure Israel should press the attack all night against the Philistines.

His priest suggested it would be wise to seek God's guidance. Would an overnight pursuit succeed? The answer was not forthcoming. There was no clear word from God!

Enraged and chagrined by the supernatural silence attending his petition, Saul flew into a fit of rage. Someone had sinned, he was sure. In blind rage he declared vehemently that the culprit must be found, and even if it was his own son, he should pay dearly with his life.

The monstrous absurdity of Saul's behavior baffles us. It scarcely seems possible Israel's king could be so spiritually inept. Almost all of his men had transgressed against God that day. It was obvious! He himself had sinned against his fellows by the extreme folly of his imposed fast. Yet now he looked for some innocent scapegoat upon whom he could place the blame for his own misdeeds.

We look on in horror as Saul calls for *Urim and Thummim* to be used in finding the offender. The outrageous monarch had forgotten that anyone who chose to discover divine guidance this way without first being sanctified themselves, would receive a false message. So when in the darkness of that dreadful night, with the campfire flames dancing up to cast weird shadows over the massed men, Jonathan's name was drawn. It was as if an evil spirit from Saul had spoken—not God.

It was true only Jonathan had tasted the honey that day. But it was equally true that only he had been totally ignorant of his father's foolish curse. He was a man, the only man present in this macabre setting, utterly innocent of any wrongdoing or sin.

Yet now in violent mental derangement Saul shouted that he be put to death. It was all a part of the man's perverse nature that the innocent should suffer to atone for the sinister evil of the lawless. The savior of his people should be punished for the gross stupidity and evil offenses of others.

Only the loyalty of his fellow warriors on this grim

night preserved Jonathan from a grisly end at his father's own ferocious hands. They insisted his life be spared from Saul. But only by a mere hair's-breadth did he escape from the twisted, tormented spirit of one totally out of touch with the Almighty.

There are stern lessons for all of us here. Far too often men and women try to pin the blame for their misfortunes on others. They look for scapegoats to bear the brunt of their own evil. Often by a pious parade of supposedly spiritual activity they endeavor to cover up their own inadequacies. It deceives no one!

We often forget the simple fact that the most godly men and women among us are the least spectacular. Like Jonathan, they are the quiet ones who in company with Christ move humbly through life achieving great things for God. Their characters are sterling, their conduct beyond reproach.

After this dreadful ordeal Saul and his people, instead of routing the enemy, scattered and returned to their homes. What might have been a momentous overthrow of the Philistines, turned out to be but an incentive for them to attack Israel again.

Word of the inconclusive battle spread to all the surrounding enemy nations. The end result was that Saul, instead of enjoying a rule of strength and peace, found himself caught up in constant conflict with the Amorites, the kings of Zobah, the Philistines, as well as Israel's ancient foes, the Amalekites.

The wars of attrition went on and on through all the years of his troubled monarchy. And, just as Samuel had warned Israel before his coronation, Saul continually recruited the finest young men he could find to reinforce his standing army.

Though Israel now had a titular monarch as head of

state, it was a disastrous exchange for the government of God Himself. The nation was in fact being ruled by a fool, whose actions were an affront to God, and a tyranny to His people.

8
Saul's Fatal Disobedience to God

Saul had been in power over Israel for about nine or ten years when Samuel again came to him with a special message from the Lord. The time had come for the Amalekites, Israel's ancient foe, to be annihilated once and for all.

It was Amalek, the ferocious offspring of Esau, who first fought against Israel at Rephidim when God delivered Israel from Egypt. While Moses prayed for his people in peril with arms outstretched to God, young Joshua and his fledgling army had triumphed over the Amalekites on the desert floor below (*see Exodus 17*).

After the first flush of victory in the wilderness wastes Israel had been warned that there would be an on-going vendetta with Amalek from generation to generation. Now for 400 years the rivalry had raged on.

So, Samuel's implicit orders were that the day had come when Israel should destroy this enemy—even to the last living person along with all their livestock. Absolutely nothing should be spared. It was a drastic decree that demanded the most implicit compliance. Saul mustered a formidable force of 200,000 footmen from Israel and 10,000 warriors from Judah. With a daring drive he swept south and west across the Negev desert as far as the outermost boundaries of Egypt. His strategy succeeded. Amalek was completely encircled!

Like a bird caught in a snare, Agag the king of Amalek and his forces fell into the hands of Saul. Only the Kenites, an offshoot of Amalek, who had been favorable to Israel in the past, were spared.

Yet in truth the annihilation of the enemy was not executed as God commanded. For Saul decided to return in triumph bringing with him Agag as a prize trophy of war. In addition his victorious forces had persuaded Saul to spare the finest of the enemy livestock as spoils from the combat. Their facetious argument was that the fine fat cattle, sheep and goats would make admirable sacrifices. The best of the camels and asses would bear home other booty that seemed far too good to destroy.

It was in direct disobedience to Jehovah's command. Saul deliberately ignored the explicit instructions of the Most High. Saul and his triumphant troops marched home in a blaze of proud and heady self-assurance. Agag was in chains and they were all richer with their spoils of war.

The rugged old prophet Samuel, keenly attuned to the Spirit of God, knew full well of Saul's action, even though he was encamped in the desert wastes. He knew Agag had been spared. He knew herds of livestock were being driven along the dusty trails back to Israel.

With anguished spirit over Saul's intransigence the old man wept before the Lord all night. Hot tears fell from his weary old eyes on behalf of the stubborn Saul.

He realized with bitter certainty that in his folly, Saul had forfeited forever his claim to the kingdom. His deliberate disobedience would mean that the monarchy would be torn from his grasp to be given to another ruler whom God would choose to supplant Saul.

Despite his agony of the long sleepless night, Samuel rose at dawn to go out and meet the returning army. Saul, flushed with his own apparent success, was in an expansive mood. He greeted Samuel with a great show of esteem and self-congratulation: *"Blessed be thou of the Lord: I have performed the commandment of the Lord!"* (1 Samuel 15:13).

Saul's brazen attempt to bluff the sage old seer only deepened Samuel's despair. He already knew much more than Saul ever guessed. The lowing of cattle and bleating of sheep in the background were confirmation of the king's calumny. He was digging himself a pit of deception that would spell his own destruction.

With the Spirit of God surging strongly through him in tremendous intensity, the prophet confronted Saul with his awful peril in disobeying God. Despite his deep personal affection for the new king, Samuel served a higher sovereign. And now he stood unshaken before the handsome giant towering over him.

"Why did you not obey the voice of God? Why did you fly upon the spoil? Why have you done such evil?" (see v. 19). His words were charged with pathos, heavy with agony. Saul pulled himself up to his full height. He appeared as a mountain of manhood overshadowing the stooped and feeble old prophet. *"I have obeyed the Lord!"* he thundered angrily. *"I have gone where he sent me, I have destroyed the Amalekites. I have brought Agag here. The people have spared livestock to sacrifice to your God"* (see vv. 20 and 21).

It was a daring, bold-faced attempt to vindicate himself. He was confident his commendable conduct far outweighed the less important fact that he had failed to carry out his commission.

But Samuel was not to be swayed. He was fearless in speaking emphatically for the Lord. He was not intimidated by the towering monarch before him. And the words which now came from his spirit were like sword thrusts plunged into Saul's stubborn soul.

"To obey is better than sacrifice, and to hearken (to God's commands) better than the fat of rams. . . . Because (you have) rejected the word of the Lord, he hath also rejected (you) from being king" (1 Samuel 15:22–23).

The bold facade had been stripped from Saul. Suddenly all his defenses were down. The stabbing impact of Samuel's declaration shattered his self-assurance.

"I have sinned," he admitted half-heartedly, without deep remorse, or profound contrition. *"But honor me with your presence as I worship your God before this people"* (see vv. 24 and 25).

Not wishing to humiliate the king in public, Samuel consented to this request. But before doing so he had turned from the distraught monarch, torn his robe in a show of despair, then proclaimed *"God has rent the kingdom from you this day and given it to a neighbor of yours who is better suited to be king"* (see v. 28).

Already Saul was a king in eclipse. In less than ten years, he had passed the zenith of his prowess with both God and men. He had strutted his stuff on the little stage of his own self-centered career. It had been a pathetic performance up to this point.

Now there stood in the wings, as it were, a courageous young shepherd high in the rough hills of Judah, waiting to take center stage in Israel's tragic history.

Before leaving Saul to fade into the tragic and ghastly twilight of his act, Samuel called for Agag to be brought before him. The wily desert fox was sure he would survive under Saul's protection. What he did not reckon on was the ruthless determination of God's prophet to perform the task assigned to Saul.

Seizing a sword in his bony hands Samuel rushed on Agag, decapitated him in fury, then hacked his sun-burned body into a mass of blood-soaked flesh. His grim action convinced Saul that he had failed God. One look was worth ten thousand words!

It was a dreadful end to Saul's spiritual leadership over Israel. Never again during his life did Samuel visit him. Instead he mourned for Saul as a son spiritually dead and now alienated from God.

The tragic sequence of events in Saul's career reveals to us in vivid clarity certain spiritual truths not well understood by many. The first of these is that in the context of biblical history, Amalek always represents our old self-life. The continuous conflict between our so-called "old nature" and the new life of God's spirit within is reflected in the ongoing struggle between Israel and Amalek.

We are called to be done with self. We are told to use violence if necessary to eliminate our worst enemy, self. Most of us, like Saul, simply will not do this. We pander to our own interests, we use subtle tactics to preserve our own identity. We will not be ruthless in actions of self-discipline, under God, to obey Him implicitly.

We prefer to play little games in which we insist we are serving Him while all the time pleasing ourselves.

In very drastic language the Lord Jesus Christ made clear what was called for in following Him. He said if your hand causes you to stumble, sever it. If your eye leads you to go astray, pluck it out. The kingdom of God is entered by struggle of soul. It is gained in all its glory only by those who are brave enough to be violent with their old self-life.

Saul never understood this. Nor do many members in the church today. Saul could not spare Agag and the spoils of Amalek and still claim to serve the Lord. Jesus said we cannot serve both God and mammon.

In Romans 6:11–14 Paul makes it abundantly clear that if we are to be conquerors in Christ, the dominion of the old self-life must be shattered. In its place must come complete surrender to God Himself.

This is an ongoing process, something accomplished daily as we submit to the supreme sovereignty of God's gracious Spirit. It calls for our complete compliance with Christ's commands. In short, to be overcomers in the conflict of our spiritual lives we must obey God's Word without debate.

Saul deluded himself when he insisted he had carried out God's wishes. He had not! And he knew it! Nor can such failure to fulfill the divine commission be compensated for by coming up with so-called sacrifices and services. They are no substitute for obedience!

Put in its plainest terms, we can say that if one wishes to rule and reign with Christ, which is His high calling to His people, it can only be achieved as He in turn rules and reigns in us. We only have power to achieve His purposes as we submit gladly to His presence at work within us.

Saul never learned this lesson. He never truly repented of his waywardness. He never fully submitted himself to God's will. He was forever a man determined to protect his own self-interests. Ultimately he simply became a pathetic castaway. His end was a dreadful alienation from God.

Samuel had given him every opportunity to succeed. Yet Saul squandered every gift from God in folly and rebellion to end in tragedy.

9

David Is Anointed to Be King

The prophet Samuel, gaunt and haggard with the grief of his twilight years, sorrowed over the wayward Saul. The new monarch was like a spiritual son to him. He was now, like Samuel's own blood sons, far away from God. All were a burden to bear, a cause for anguish of spirit to the grand old man of God.

In the midst of his mourning a startling word of new hope and bright cheer came from the Lord. Samuel was to fill his horn with fresh oil, set out at once for Bethlehem to the household of Jesse, and there anoint one of Jesse's sons as the new sovereign in Israel.

The divine instruction of the Most High was that Samuel should still be His flaming servant. All the distress over Saul and his own willful sons should never impede his availability to the purposes of God. If anything, it was Samuel's godly sorrow that kept him humble in heart and contrite in spirit. Such people God loves to lift up and use in noble service.

Without delay, nor debating the issue, Samuel, it would seem, should have been glad to go at once. But he was not, for he feared Saul's ferocious jealousy. He trembled at the thought of the monarch's black, brooding moods. A man who was willing to slay his own son Jonathan in a rage would not hesitate to behead an old man with a blow from his sword.

But the command from the Almighty could not be denied. Samuel had to go! So, driving a young heifer before him as a sure sign that he came in peace, Samuel went to Bethlehem. The local residents were terror-stricken. They had heard of Samuel's burning zeal for God's honor as he rushed on Agag and hacked him to death. What was his mission now? These were tempestuous times in the land. The nation was in upheaval!

With outstretched arms and warm eyes Samuel spoke reassuringly to the wary elders of the country village. He was there to offer peace offerings to Jehovah. He was there on a divine assignment. He invited the heads of all the households to join him in the ritual of sanctifying themselves before the Lord. They were to be a special people set apart for a special purpose—the selection of a new sovereign king.

Family by family they came. Finally Jesse and seven of his stalwart sons stood in awe before the ancient seer. In low tones, barely above a whisper, Samuel spoke softly as Eliab the first-born looked into his eyes—"Surely this one is the Lord's anointed!"

But it was not to be. The man of God's choosing was not to be appraised by his outward appearance or personal charisma. In fact, the severe rebuke that came clearly to Samuel on this momentous occasion was *The Lord seeth not as man seeth: for man looketh on the outward appearance, but the Lord looketh on the heart*" (1 Samuel 16:2).

God was determined He would have a man whose will

was set to do His will. This was the ultimate criterion for kingship.

Son by son, all seven of Jesse's older boys passed before Samuel in steady succession. Any one of them, it seemed, was of such outstanding stature that they could well have served as a successor to Saul. Yet it was not to be.

Momentarily at a loss what to do next, the aged prophet may have wondered if he had come on a fool's errand. Prompted by God's Spirit to press on, he then asked Jesse if perchance he might still have another son not present. Quickly the old saint was assured that David, the youngest lad in the family, was out on the range tending a flock of sheep.

"Send and fetch him at once," Samuel ordered. He would not sit down or rest his weary frame until his mission was accomplished for the Lord. He was determined to carry out his charge without delay.

When David came in from the hills there was about him a splendid aura of young manhood at its best. Fresh air, sunshine and the spartan life of a shepherd had bronzed his body, hardened his strong muscles and brightened his beautiful eyes. He bore himself with strength, grace and ease. All of this was bound up in youthful zest and gracious good will.

Immediately Samuel knew the special man of God's own choice stood before him. Here was Israel's second sovereign. Here stood her Shepherd King.

"At last, Samuel, this is my man. Anoint him for special service!" The Lord spoke clearly (see 1 Samuel 16:12).

As the stooped patriarch stretched himself on tiptoe to pour his horn of oil over David's dark and shining locks, he little dreamed of the youth's incredible destiny under God. Here was a youth called from the solitude of the hills, from the humble care of sheep, from a quiet life of stark simplicity to become the greatest monarch Israel would ever know.

No, God does not see as man sees. He does not measure character by charisma. He does not defer to human values. God's chief criterion for selecting special servants for mighty purposes is: *"Are you willing to do My will?"* This is the acid test. Despite all of an individual's other failings, if above all else his one consuming desire is to be *"a man after God's own heart (will),"* he will be lifted above the turmoil of his times, in great honor.

This was to be true for David. Despite his mistakes; despite his personal disasters; despite the awesome ordeals of his later life; he was to emerge as one whose life would be a benediction to millions across thousands of years of human history.

God's gracious Spirit came upon the young shepherd in rich measure as the sweet olive oil shone upon his head, face and shoulders. He was the son of Jesse, a son of Judah, an offspring of Jacob (Israel), Isaac and Abraham. More than that he stood strong in the great tradition and lineage of Israel, through whom eventually the Savior of all the world would come to earth.

In this same village of Bethlehem, in the same fields and range from which David had been called, in the same sheltering sheepfold where he had corralled his sheep would come those cataclysmic words from on high: *"For unto you is born this day in the city of David a Savior, which is Christ the Lord!"* (Luke 2:11)

It would be well over a thousand years before that happened. For nearly eleven hundred years the offspring of this newly anointed Shepherd King would await the appearance of a sure sign that the *Great Good Shepherd* of all time, the King of all kings, the promised *Messiah, Emmanuel, "God with us,"* was among men.

His mission accomplished, Samuel returned in peace

and quietness to his home in Ramah. By contrast David was now suddenly to be thrust into a life of great adventure and dire peril. To the end of his long years he would know only war, bloodshed and enormous anguish of spirit. Yet out of such unpromising material God would bring tremendous honor, fame, wealth, blessing and beauty of language never matched in another human being.

The foundation for such a future under God's great hand had been laid in the stern and severe solitude of David's life as a shepherd. Alone, with his young spirit open and sensitive to the Spirit of God, there had come to him clearly the sterling concepts of inner integrity and personal uprightness which he must show in the king's court.

Even though for years yet to come, David would be flung into furious interaction with the tyranny of Saul, the sense of God's Spirit with him never departed. Always David was a man receptive to the word of the Lord, ready to repent of his wrongs, eager above all else to do God's will. In this he and Saul were poles apart—as different as the bright sun reflected from his sun-kissed face and the black moods that engulfed the sinister soul of Saul.

The record given to us is that in fact the Spirit of God, grieved and quenched by Saul's intransigence, departed from him. Instead there overtook him an evil spirit of such a dreadful disposition that even his associates knew he needed help.

Like so many moderns they assumed music and other mental therapy would cure his condition. What they missed altogether was that Saul's melancholy was more than mere depression. It was the deep dark sign of inner sin for which he would never repent . . . and from which he could never recover in any other way.

So it was decided to search for a superb musician, someone who by playing soft, sweet melodies on a harp, could
bring some relief to Saul's madness. The choice fell on
young David. Word had reached Saul's court that the
sturdy shepherd, along with his other outstanding attributes, was also a fine harpist.

It was also reported to the king that David, though
only a youth, was an unusual character of remarkable
courage. His associates knew well of his fearlessness in
protecting his father's flock. He was not afraid to tackle
any predator, be it lion, bear or human raider. Apparently, too, when he was given a chance he was valiant
in battle, yet not foolhardy or rash. He had proven himself
to be a persistent and wise young man Perhaps best of
all it was quite apparent God's presence was always with
him.

With such a high recommendation Saul sent for the
sturdy shepherd. And when the young countryman stood
before the king there was an immediate attraction for
him. In fact it could be said in modern language, "It
was love at first sight." For not only did Saul show a
great fondness for David, he immediately appointed him
to be his personal armorbearer.

The sudden transition from being a solitary sheep man
on the dry, hot rangeland around Bethlehem to the favorite of the king's court did not unbalance David. He was
not a man given to personal pride. He was not swayed
by the star status thrust upon him. Eventually he was
himself called to be a stalwart servant both to his God
and to his king.

When Saul was in deep depression David played for
him.

When Saul went into combat, David bore his war gear.

When Saul relaxed, David was a friend to him and

his family. As time went on he became one of the dearest associates Jonathan had ever known. Like a fresh rain from the hills David brought rich blessings into the dry desolation of Saul's life and home.

10

Goliath Challenges Israel

Slowly the uncertain years of Saul's unsteady rule unfolded. As Samuel had foretold, Israel's king had spent most of his energies in pandering to his own royal interests. The ancient enemies surrounding his nation had not been subdued. Thus Israel was highly vulnerable to attack.

Young David, too, had led a most unsettling sort of life. Part of the time he served in Saul's presence. Part of the time he tended his father's flock of sheep that grazed the desert range. He was becoming fully at ease in the royal court, yet, at the same time he was hardening into a tough, wilderness man.

Then suddenly the restive Philistines, from the southwest borders of Israel, decided to launch a major attack on Israel. Since the desperate days when they had been routed by Jonathan's fierce assault, they had regained their strength as a people and now regrouped their fighting men into a formidable army. It was time to avenge themselves on their adversary.

A huge force of warriors moved into Judah. There they

encamped in *Ephesdammim,* the so-called *"Valley of Blood."*

A small, shining stream ran through the valley floor. On one slope stood the armies of the enemy, and on the other were ranged the forces of Saul. Each side put on a bold show of might. The fighting men would march and countermarch back and forth as if challenging one another to combat.

For Israel, however, the presence of the Philistines was more terrifying because there were huge men in their ranks. These were the descendants of the *Anakim,* the giants who had struck terror into the first spies sent into Canaan by Moses some 400 years before. Now once again the men of Israel may have felt like mere "grasshoppers" in their presence.

This was especially true when they heard the ringing challenges of Goliath, a monster man clad in iron mail, echo across the valley. Basing our calculations on the most conservative values of ancient measurements, the giant was at least nine feet two inches tall. His armor weighed no less than 125 pounds. The head of his massive spear weighed fifteen pounds, the equivalent of a modern sledgehammer.

Ominously Goliath clanked back and forth across the slope shouting imprecations against Israel—defying their men to send over a champion to meet him in mortal combat. If he, the Philistine, prevailed then all Israel should fall prey to his people. If the warrior from Israel won, the reverse would be true.

It was a perilous time for God's people. As was his habit, Saul, Israel's most notable giant who towered head and shoulders above his peers, simply sat in the cool shade of his tent pitched beneath the acacia trees of Elah. He was too terrified to pick up the enemy challenge, too intimidated to go to the attack, too fearful to move. No longer imbued with God's Spirit, he stood impotent before the enemy.

What was true for Saul was in large measure also true for his men. As goes the leader, so go his followers. So for forty dreadful days Goliath stormed and raged across the slopes. His overpowering might struck sheer terror into Israel's troops.

What was transpiring in the *"Valley of Blood"* was a drama that has been acted out in a thousand ways against God's people across the centuries. The "giants" who come against the Lord's own people come in many guises. Their challenges and attacks come in various forms. But always the battle lines are drawn between righteousness and evil—for the enemies of God are bent on blood.

So often, it seems, the people of God appear almost powerless before the foe. It is as if they are paralyzed with apprehension. Most are too intimidated to join battle with the forces of evil ranged against them. Then God's Spirit moves in power and great energy upon some one person who will dare to meet the challenge.

In this moment of Israel's national emergency, the person prepared by God was young David. He was to be the one energized by the Spirit of the Most High to rescue His people from their peril.

His older brothers were away from home, long since recruited into Saul's standing army. David was the one left behind with his aged father Jesse to care for the stock. But Jesse was restless and concerned for the welfare of his sons in battle. Laden with gifts of food for them, and cheese for their officers, David was sent to find out how they fared.

To many moderns, especially those of the younger generation, it must come as a severe shock to see David's implicit obedience to his father. Here was a young man of great gifts and unusual abilities, still willing to carry out Jesse's wishes. He did not debate the issue of appearing to his brothers as a mere servant sent on a menial mission. If that was his father's desire he would do it.

God's sixth great commandment given to Israel centuries before had been: *"Honor thy father and thy mother; that thy days may be long upon the land which the Lord thy God giveth thee"* (Exodus 20:12).

This David did without dispute. At dawn he was on his way to the Valley of Blood to find out what had become of his brothers. Quickly he found the commissariat and left his gift of food rations there.

Then boldly he worked his way into the battle lines to find Eliab and his other brothers. Moving swiftly from company to company David was shocked to hear the unanswered challenges of Goliath ringing across the valley.

Was there no one daring enough in Israel to take on this gross giant who defied the armies of the Lord? Was there no warrior ready to risk his life for the honor of God and country? Was everyone paralyzed with fear? David could scarcely credit the low morale and blank terror of Saul's men who fled like frightened sheep at the approach of Goliath.

He simply could not believe what he saw!

From battle group to battle group David hurried searching for his brothers. The Israeli units were massed in their thousands upon the sun-blasted slopes, yet none dared join battle with the proud Philistines. Not one was brave enough to descend the slope, cross the stream and rush the foe in ferocious combat.

This was doubly surprising to David for he soon learned that Saul had offered an enormous bounty to any man who slew Goliath. The king had promised a handsome prize of money, the hand of his daughter in marriage and total tax exemption for the rest of the victor's life.

But even with such handsome rewards, the warriors of Israel refused to attack. Like timid children they cringed in alarm while Goliath ranted and raved against them and their God. The whole scene stirred David to the depths. His spirit, sensitive to God's Spirit, could not be silent. He was beside himself with passion for the honor of his people and the glory of his God.

Who is this foul Philistine that he should dare to defy the armies of the Most High? he wondered.

His voice taut with anger, his face flushed with the thought of battle, the adrenalin pouring into his blood stream, the young shepherd bounded from platoon to platoon. Not only was he searching for his brothers, he was also searching for some man bold enough to do battle with the foe.

At last he came on Eliab! The older brother was not that excited to see David. The precocious young stalwart had always been a pain to his more stodgy siblings. A score of jealous and hostile emotions swept through Eliab. In rapid, stabbing sentences Eliab lashed out at his brother: *"Why are you here? Where did you leave your little band of sheep? Who is caring for them? What do you know about war, to be here?"* (see 1 Samuel 17:28).

Each command was a sharp insult to David. Each was intended to shatter his self-assurance. Each was a put-down for the only person who would dare to charge into combat against Goliath on this cataclysmic day.

The taunts did not deter David. He was not to be cowed by his brother's caustic tongue and acid envy. Without engaging in an empty diatribe with Eliab he simply asked softly, *"What have I done that is amiss? Is there not a cause here great enough to consume a man?"* (see v. 29).

What happened to the young shepherd happens all too often in the life of anyone determined to do God's will, to serve His cause. Again and again those who will dare to face the foe, to lock battle with the forces of evil, find themselves harassed by their own family or friends.

In fact, our Lord warned us emphatically this would happen to anyone who followed Him (Matthew 10:29–42). And those who oppose the ardent disciples of God Himself are sometimes the very saints who are supposedly in the forefront of the struggle with evil. It is all a bit difficult.

In dismay David turned from his brothers. He kept asking the same searching question, *"Who will go against Goliath?"* Someone had to go. If necessary, someone would have to dare to die. The battle simply could not be lost by default!

David himself would attack the giant!

There was no further holding back! He would go!

Hastily the youth was brought before King Saul. The towering monarch, fully outfitted in iron armor, looked down on David with a certain air of contempt. What could a simple country lad like this do in battle?

"You can't fight Goliath. You are too young. You aren't battle-trained. The giant is a combat veteran" (see v. 33).

David was not about to be deterred by Saul. With blazing eyes and clenched fists he looked up at the king and replied in steady tones: *"Let no man's heart fail him for fear! I will charge Goliath! The Lord God who delivered me when I slew both the lion and the bear that came to raid my flock, will also preserve me from the power of this Philistine!"* (see v. 37).

This calm, unshakable declaration of quiet confidence in God silenced Saul. All his specious arguments and feeble excuses were blown away in the wind of God's Spirit who swept so strongly through David's spirit.

One man, in company with his God, could turn the tide of fear that overwhelmed a whole army, an entire nation and its feckless king. He would go in the power of the Almighty.

11

David Destroys the Giant

It is a supreme irony that Saul, who should have been Israel's natural challenger to the giant Goliath, refused to risk his own life. He, the king, was by far the biggest man in the kingdom. He was one of the few fully equipped with a complete suit of iron mail and forged weapons, all of which had come from Philistine armor-makers. Even if Saul had elected not to attack Goliath with such conventional battle gear, he had the unique advantage of a Benjaminite. This tiny tribe, a mere remnant in Israel, was the most skilled in the use of the sling to slay their foes. So without ever engaging in hand-to-hand combat with Goliath, Saul could have chosen to try and kill the giant with a stone.

But he would not!

He was too much of a coward!

Instead he preferred to let David go in his stead.

With an absurd show of fake concern for the young man's safety, the fickle king insisted David put on his massive armor. It was a ludicrous gesture reflecting Saul's deranged mentality. The strong, virile young man from the wilderness was bound and cramped by the rigid metal armor that encased his lithe muscles. It was as if he were entombed in iron—the iron forged by the enemy Philistines themselves.

"I cannot go with these!" David exclaimed, putting off the armor.

There is a powerful parallel here in the ongoing battles that God's people face in every generation. All too often those entrusted with leadership, like King Saul, have been fully equipped and armed with trappings taken from the world that opposes them.

It is assumed that the techniques and technology forged by human minds and devised by man's methods will suffice to do battle with the forces of evil. Too long, and far too often, misguided leaders try to cramp and constrict their people in the impediments of human design. We become so organized, so structured, so encased with rigid rules we cannot move forward with God.

David would have none of this!

Turning from Saul with a swift motion, the sturdy shepherd swept up his rod and staff from the ground; he slung his sheepskin bag over his sunburned shoulder; then he strode off toward the little singing stream in the valley floor, sling in hand.

It could well be he even whistled with glee as he stooped by the brook, pausing to carefully select five small, smooth stones from its murmuring waters. Not a shred of fear clouded his consciousness. He was a man strong, free and confident in his natural setting.

The blue vault of the burning sky overhead; the warm breeze of air flowing down the valley floor; the brittle sharp light of the sun on the slopes—these were all familiar to him. But most important, too, was the reassuring presence of God's Spirit resting on his spirit. This contest was God's, not just his!

With a quick bound David leaped across the stream. Alone, yet not alone, bold and rugged, he stood on enemy ground. Goliath's challenger had come. At last after forty days and forty nights of insults and oaths the giant's jeers would be flung back in his own spittlestained beard.

Seeing the bare-legged youth advance toward him Goliath burst out in more abusive language:

"Am I but a mongrel that you come against me with a shepherd's gear?" he scoffed, the sounds rumbling from behind his metal visor. *"I will give your carcass to the vultures and the jackals"* (see 1 Samuel 17:43, 44).

In an outpouring of crude and vile blasphemy, of which military men are often violent masters, Goliath heaped abuse on David. With insults, disdain and rising anger he tried to intimidate his challenger.

But David was not deterred by the diatribe.

He was not to be cowed by the curses.

Wild threats were but empty words.

David seemed utterly oblivious to the ranked armies of both Israel and the enemy which ranged over the surrounding hills like a blanket of humanity. He did not seem to see the formidable center stage of the giant amphitheater upon which he now moved as a leading character.

All he saw were his own sure hands quietly fitting a small stone into the well-worn cup of the leather sling.

He saw the exposed forehead above the giant's angry face as the crucial target for his aim.

He was himself cloaked in the presence of the Most High God. He was enfolded in the power of His Spirit. The hand and honor and skill of the Almighty were upon him. The battle was against God who sustained him.

Without being either brazen or bombastic David advanced steadily. In clear, loud, ringing syllables he shouted back: *"You come against me with a spear, a sword and a shield . . . but I come in the name and majesty of the Lord God of Israel whom you have defied!"* (see v. 45).

It was a moment of tension. For a few brief seconds silence swept across the scene. Only the soft singing of the stream could be heard. But all of Israel's army and all of the Philistines had heard David's ringing challenge.

He alone had dared to descend to that brook. He alone had dared to draw his arsenal of stones from it. He alone had dared to leap across it in open assault on the enemy.

The brook, like the ever-flowing will of God, is what separated the two armies. The will of God is ever the source of a godly person's strength. The will of God is that which decides whether or not we will go on to great exploits for the Lord.

Most of us will not plunge into it, or draw from it.

Many of us never dare to see it as our source of strength.

Pausing for a few more moments, David cried out in clear, ringing tones: *"This day the Lord will deliver you into my hand. The battle is the Lord's. All the earth will know that there is a living God in Israel"* (see v. 46).

The staccato shouts were like bugle notes for battle. The blood raced in his veins. The light of victory gleamed in his bright eyes. A grin creased his flushed face: *"In God's might I will smite you. I will take your head from your shoulders. I will provide the buzzards and scavengers with a grisly banquet of Philistine carcasses. God will give you into our hands"* (see v. 46).

With a rush, like a leopard leaping to the attack, David launched himself up the hill toward Goliath. The sling whistled ominously as he whirled it over his head. Then the thong was released. The stone struck!

The next instant the giant crashed down the slope,

face forward. The blood spurted from the skull shattered by the rock. It was as if he had been struck by a bullet.

David rushed up to the prostrate form as Goliath's armorbearer fled in panic. Picking up the giant's massive sword he severed his head, the blood and gore spurting from the jugular vein.

In triumph David stood upon the huge hulk. The battle was over! The daring deed was done! It was an instant of intense elation for all Israel. It drew all her fighting men into ferocious action. The Philistines fled in wild panic and total disarray.

What all of Saul's military might had been unable to achieve, a single shepherd had done with simple faith in God.

Faith is a person's own personal, private response to the Word of God in the character of Christ (the Lord), to the point where they will act upon it in obedience. It is much more than mere belief. It is perfectly possible for a man or woman to believe much of God's declared will, yet never do it. The result is impotence!

All of Israel's warriors and Saul himself believed they should have joined battle with the enemy and driven the invader from their soil. But none of them did. Not one would go against Goliath!

The secret of David's success was that not only did he believe the battle was the Lord's (and that in the case of the Almighty he would be preserved from harm), but he was bold enough to step out of the ranks and actually attack the giant. This is faith in action! God preserves His people as they press the conflict. God does His part. He calls upon us to do our share!

This David recounts so clearly in his hymns of praise recorded in such Psalms as 23, 46 and 64. He is a man whose calm confidence is in God—not in man. It is in the Almighty that he finds a cause to live for at any cost. In the Lord he finds his very life.

The destruction of Goliath and rout of the entire Philistine army was a high point in David's career. No wonder the women and girls of Israel would dance and sing to one another: *"Saul has slain his thousands, but David his ten thousands"* (1 Samuel 18:7).

It had taken patience and perseverance for David to reach this pinnacle of prominence. Some six slow, grinding, frustrating years had crept past since the day Samuel had anointed him to be king over Israel—years replete with reproaches from his family, condescension from Saul whom he served and insults from the enemy.

Little did David realize how hard and rough the trail of tears would be that he had yet to tramp. Little did he know how terrible Saul's cruel tyranny would be— how vicious his jealousy and how bitter his rage against this one who that day delivered Israel from despair.

Saul's first deranged action after the triumph was to demand that David be brought before him. In stinging, absurd questions he demanded to know who David was, where he came from, and who his father was—as if he did not even recognize the youth who had so often played to appease his moods! As if he did not even know this one who had been his own armorbearer!

In his selfish madness of mind Saul was more concerned with who should marry his daughter, than giving honor to Israel's new hero. Saul with his convoluted, hot emotions was setting the stage for a diabolical vendetta against David.

12
Saul's Jealous Rage Against David

Though the Philistines had fled in stark terror after Goliath's death, they had not been totally destroyed. The Israelis under Saul seemed incapable of a complete conquest. Instead, they were more intent on returning to raid and loot the enemy tents left behind in wild abandon.

Even David himself saw to it that the giant's armor should be stripped from his carcass and kept as a trophy of war. The severed, gory head of the slain giant was taken to Jerusalem as a supreme humiliation. Why we do not know, for Jerusalem was an enemy stronghold held by the Jebusites.

Meanwhile Saul insisted that the shepherd should no longer return to Bethlehem to tend his sheep. He was to become a royal resident of his court. Jonathan was thrilled to have his friend so close at hand.

In a gracious gesture of esteem, honor and good will Jonathan, the natural heir to Saul's throne, took off his princely robe and put it on David. More than that, he garbed the rough outdoorsman in his own royal wardrobe. The final touch of his profound affection was to equip David with his own armor.

Rather than having a sense of rivalry for the one Samuel had anointed to supplant him, Jonathan showed only profound respect. It was a mark of a generous spirit. This was in fact that special dimension of selfless love that is the hallmark of anyone upon whom God's Spirit rests. It is in truth the very love of God eloquently expressed in a human life.

For his part, David did not parade himself before the public to win their popular applause. He was wise enough to remain subservient to his king. His exploits would speak for themselves. Coupled with his quiet reserve, his humility quickly won the hearts of the nation as a popular hero.

Probably in response to this national adulation, Saul appointed David to be commander-in-chief of all his fighting men. It was a flash in the pan idea. For as word of David's thrilling victory swept across the hills and valleys, the women and girls everywhere began to dance and chant his praises.

"Saul has slain his thousands! But David has vanquished his ten thousands!"

The theme of triumph and adoration enraged Saul. His twisted emotions burned with flaming jealousy. Instead of taking pride in Israel's deliverance through David's hand, he saw the young man now only as a deadly archrival. Saul's humiliation in the songs and dances of the girls degenerated to hostility, then violent hatred, for David.

A dark, morose, angry mood settled upon his soul. Deep depression engulfed the king's spirit. With burning malice he saw David as one destined to capture the loyalty of Israel and so supplant him as their sovereign. He would never let this happen if he could prevent it. In a fit of rage David was summoned to come and play the harp for him.

Saul, like one demented, ranted and raved in torment of spirit. He, who at the outset of his rule had prophesied among the prophets, was now but a raging mouthpiece for the forces of evil that controlled him.

David's hands moved softly over the harp strings. The sweet melodies that before had stilled Saul's anguished soul only seemed to arouse him more.

Suddenly the king grasped a javelin from his side and hurled it with deadly intent at David. In a split second the harpist ducked. The shining shaft quivered in the wall a few inches above his head. A few moments later a second spear whistled toward him. In a quick reflex of strong muscles David escaped by a hair.

It was enough!

Saul's deadly intentions were clear.

There could be no peace or safety in his presence.

Saul feared David with stark terror because he recognized the presence of the Lord upon him. David, in turn, feared Saul because of the evil spirit which oppressed the monarch.

Under this sort of wretched tyranny, not only would Saul become an individual of terrible outrages, but he would make David's life a grim ordeal. The consequences would be sorrow, calamity and tension for both men.

Saul's fiercest attack on David was not with a weapon of iron held in his hand. It was an act of humiliation by a demotion in rank. From being commander-in-chief over the armies of Israel and Judah, David was reduced to the low rank of a captain over a single regiment of men.

Instead of rebelling against such unwarranted discrimination, David accepted the king's orders with equanimity. It speaks much for the young man that he chose to act discreetly in the face of such provocation rather than try to rally public support to his side. Little wonder David was regarded so highly as an unusually wise young leader in Israel. For this he became a national favorite, loved by all.

This swing in popularity only served to infuriate Saul further. His angry hostility began to feed on its own self-pity. He knew only outrage and insult because of David's quiet fame among the people. His convoluted emotions began to devise other diabolical schemes for destroying the innocent young man who up until now had done him nothing but good.

In an outworking of knavery and deception of the first magnitude we are horrified by the depths of chicanery to which Saul descended. He had become a virtual mad-man bent on only one vicious end. He would do away with David. He would brook no rival in his realm. He would have David's head at any cost!

What Saul did not know, nor do many today, is that jealousy is one of the most destructive of all sins. It is a grim evil against God, others and ourselves.

Jealousy is too often brushed aside as a fickle human weakness. It is much much more than that, for it bears within it five fatal downward steps to ultimate terror and destruction. Here they are, each beginning with the letter H to help us remember them:

HURT—a feeling of personal insult or injury.
HOSTILITY—leading to a need for self-preservation.
HATE—deep anger and animosity toward others.
HARM—taking action to injure someone.
HELL—alienation from God and men.

The ancient Indian tribes of the north summed it up this way: *"The hated one looks upon the hater and watches him destroy himself."*

This was the perilous path upon which Saul had now set his feet. He would never truly repent of his evil intentions. He would never turn from his wicked ways. He would seal his own self-destruction.

His next cruel move was to defraud David of the right to his own daughter's hand in marriage. It was common knowledge all across the country that whoever slew Goliath would be given the king's eldest daughter as a bride. Saul now reneged on that promise. So the promised *Merab* was instead given to another man.

This was a blatant insult. It was designed to humiliate David among his compatriots. But the outcome was to the young man's advantage; now he would have opportunity to marry *Michal* who truly loved him as a national hero.

When word came to the king that a deep affection for David burned within his daughter's heart, he literally rubbed his hands in glee. Here was his chance to lure David into a death trap. Michal could be used as the bait to risk his very life to win her love. What the lion, the bear, the giant Goliath and his own sharp javelins could not do, a woman's love could accomplish.

Saul sent a tempting message to the sturdy young hero. *"If you want Michal as your bride, bring me no dowry except the foreskins of a hundred Philistines"* (see v. 25).

It was a crude and cunning offer, gross and debased as the one who sent it. Saul was sure beyond any doubt that in collecting the "scalps," so to speak, of a hundred enemy warriors, David would be killed in the attempt. Saul reasoned that David's romance with Michal would make him so reckless he would gladly lose his life for her love. Saul was certain that this would be a suicide mission for his archrival.

But it was not to be.

On the contrary, David picked up the scheme with pleasure. He would accept the terms with glad abandon.

It was a challenge that stirred his spirit and quickened his pulse.

Gathering a band of eager comrades around him, David promptly set off in search of Philistine victims.

He was bound to have his beautiful bride at the fearsome cost of hand-to-hand combat with the enemy. What were a hundred casualties? In his ardor and daring the flaming young giant-killer came back with two hundred gory tokens of those slain.

One by one the double tally of foreskins were laid out in open view before the demented Saul. Stripped of all excuses, shamed by David's show of force, silenced before his people, the king was forced to give Michal to the man he dreaded most in all the world.

The tables had been turned on Saul! His best-laid schemes had back-fired. His insidious devices had only worked out to David's greater honor. Now suddenly this arch foe had become his own son-in-law, a veritable member of his own family.

It only added to Saul's chagrin.

It seemed he simply could not win.

In his own inner darkness he detected in some obscure degree that he really was fighting against more than a mere man. He was in conflict with almighty God, for His presence and His power rested upon David in obvious measure.

This terrorized Saul. His outrage and hostility were against David. Yet his personal vendetta was against God. In actual fact he found himself opposed by God's Spirit.

As for Israel as a nation, David, so handsome, so wise, so valiant, and his beautiful princess had become the darlings of the people. They were royal favorites.

13

David Is Driven to Flee to Samuel

The immense popularity David enjoyed with the people infuriated Saul. His selfish spirit and angry emotions were inflamed with jealousy. His animosity and belligerence knew no bounds. The brighter the younger man's reputation shone among his people, the darker and more hideous became Saul's belligerence.

In blind fury he ordered both Jonathan and all his servants to murder David at the earliest opportunity. He was determined to do away with his rival in outright violence. But he had not reckoned on Jonathan's loyalty to his friend.

Jonathan, too, had faced the senseless fury of his father. He knew what it was to have his very life in jeopardy at the hands of this deranged man. Still he would not be intimidated by the king's wrath.

Jonathan alerted David to flee into the nearby fields and go into hiding. At a prearranged spot he would also take his demented father aside and plead with him for clemency. If ever there was a peacemaker it was this noble prince in Israel. Of him it surely could be said, "He is a child of God."

Respectfully, yet forcefully, Jonathan entreated his father to face the facts. David had never done him any harm. The young shepherd warrior had risked his very life to deliver both Saul and his army from the Philistines and their giant.

More than this, Jonathan reminded the king that all of David's service to him had been above reproach. He soothed him with his music. He served him as a loyal armorbearer. He commanded his fighting men with great bravery and outstanding success.

"Why then do you want to sin against this noble servant by slaying him? You want to shed innocent blood without a cause!" (see 1 Samuel 19:5).

Jonathan's defense of David seemed, momentarily at least, to sink into Saul's darkened soul. Somehow he seemed to sense the awful solemnity of his bitter and groundless anger against a good man. So in a sudden outburst of vehemence he made a complete turn around and swore that David would be spared. The tragedy of it all was that Saul never knew true repentance. He never truly saw the gravity of his terrible evil against God and man. He never turned in utter disgust from the desperate outrage of his own sinister selfishness.

His apparent forbearance, however, was sufficiently convincing that Jonathan persuaded David to return to the king's court as before. At least it was a temporary reprieve. Once again it appeared harmony had been restored in the kingdom.

Jonathan's courage in confronting his father presents a powerful principle of godly behavior which demands our attention. At great risk to himself, both physically and emotionally, Jonathan had challenged Saul's conduct.

The unpredictable king could well have become so enraged he would have slain his own son. Or he may have felt so insulted as to banish him from his presence forever. Jonathan's stern and forthright judgment of his father's sin and folly was a high risk action. But it was honored by God, for it produced peace.

This class of godly courage is seldom seen. All too often people prefer to hide behind the excuse that we are not to judge another. They forget, it seems, that the people of God are clearly instructed to judge all things (*see 1 Corinthians* 2:14–16).

It is expected of us that, though we are not to condemn others, we are to be bold enough to pass judgment on evil actions and wrong behavior. We are given clear guidelines in God's Word as to what is right and what is wrong—what is noble and what is deplorable. We Christians do not live in a gray world of shadows and uncertainty. We are people of sharp enlightenment. We must be brave enough, as Jonathan was, to live in that light and call sin what it is!

Unfortunately the temporary truce that prevailed between David and his monarch was short-circuited. The Philistines, like insatiable predators, again attacked Israel. War broke out and again David and his warriors went into furious counteraction. As before, there was a tremendous slaughter of the enemy, and again David returned in triumph.

It was too much for the tormented king. Jealousy, rivalry, evil imaginations engulfed his fevered temper. Oppressed by an evil spirit, he burned with black anger. His soul was scorched with the acid of his own horrible animosity.

David was summoned before him to play his harp. The first, few, flowing chords had scarcely filled the royal chambers when Saul suddenly hurled a spear across the room. With instant reflexes David ducked. The glittering shaft struck the wall beside him. In a flash he could have seized the quivering weapon and plunged it through Saul's silken robes.

Instead, the long-suffering shepherd slipped swiftly from the room. Under cover of night he sped through the darkness to the sanctuary of his home with Michal.

But there was no safety there! Michal, like her brother Jonathan, knew all too well the madness of her father's melancholy moods. She was sure the house would be surrounded with armed men ordered to destroy David at break of day.

Secretly she lowered her husband from a remote window in the dark. Like a hunted hart he would flee through the night into exile from his family. It was a desperate escape.

Michal, for her part, had learned the art of deception from her father. His capacity for duplicity and strange intrigue had been passed on to her. She too was full of folly.

When Saul's soldiers demanded David's surrender at dawn, she insisted that he was ill in bed.

A second time the fuming king sent word that David be delivered to him in his bed. When this was done it was to discover that his daughter had double-crossed him by putting a carved idol under the covers with a pillow of goat's hair at the head.

In an outburst of fury Saul ranted against Michal for daring to deceive him. Again she lied, claiming her husband had threatened to kill her if she did not help him to escape.

This was a brazen betrayal of her husband. It was a cruel, cunning move that turned away her father's wrath from her. It was a crafty scheme that saved her skin but strained the marriage. She had forfeited not only the loss of her beloved, but every hope she may ever have had of becoming a queen in Israel.

The price of dishonesty is high indeed.

One does not indulge in deception without irreparable damage to one's soul. What Michal had watched her father do again and again in his grim vendetta with David, she now was doing herself. And for both her and her sire the end results would be disaster intertwined with unrelenting despair.

Deception is not something which can be merely brushed aside as human weakness. It is a destructive habit that eventually demolishes the one who indulges in it.

In bold contrast to the trickery of Michal, David now sought for the strong counsel of a great man of God. He needed more than human comfort. He longed above all else for the sure guidance of God's Spirit—the calm reassurance that his sure hope was in God.

In his extremity he did not go back to his home village of Bethlehem. He did not return to his own father Jesse, or his brothers. Nor did he ever feel drawn back to the wild hills and clean wind of his beloved sheep country.

Instead, David went to find Samuel, the venerated old prophet of the Most High. Samuel, who had been a spiritual mentor to Saul, would now likewise become a spiritual mentor to David. He would take just as much time and trouble instructing this young successor to Israel's throne as he had the first king. Not only would David become the military leader for his people, but also their spiritual shepherd.

Samuel, when he withdrew from Saul after slaying Agag, had not faded away into oblivion. Rather he had returned to Ramah, his favorite area of the country, and there gathered around him an energetic and zealous group of young men who were under his tutelage as prophets. Eventually they would take his place as leaders in the spiritual affairs of the nation.

Here David found respite from Saul's harassment. And here Samuel encouraged David in his communion with God. It is thought that some of David's most moving poems were written at Naioth in Ramah, especially those like Psalms 41, 42 and 119 which recount the power of God to preserve His own, and the sure guidance of His Word, if obeyed.

In wondrous ways David had seen the arm of the Almighty displayed in real-life situations to deliver him. He had been spared from the lion, the bear, the giant Goliath, the enemy Philistines, the attacks of Saul and every agent set against him.

David had discovered that *"A man is immortal as long as God has work for him to do in this world."*

Yet even here in company with Samuel it seemed his life hung by a hair. Three times, in rapid succession, Saul sent armed units to arrest David. Each time when they came in sight of Samuel and his young associates, the king's men came under the impact of God's Presence in that place. Instead of taking David by force they fell under the power of God's Spirit and began to prophesy as the others did.

In sheer frustration Saul himself set off for Ramah to vent his fury on his quarry. It was a foolish act. For he, too, fell upon the ground. He tore off his royal robe and lay prostrate in the dust. It is not certain whether his utterances were from God or from the evil spirit which oppressed him.

Obviously even his contemporaries could not be sure, for they asked in awe: *"Is Saul also among the prophets?"* (see v. 24). His diabolical behavior did little to confirm such a conclusion.

14

David and Jonathan's Friendship

Even though David was in Samuel's company at Ramah, once Saul found him there, he no longer felt secure. In desperation, like a deer hounded in the hunt, he again fled for his life.

David, strange to say, still did not return to his home at Bethlehem or the security of the wilderness he knew so well. He chose rather to return to see Jonathan, his dearest friend. Somehow he needed to be reassured that he could survive the assaults of the mad king. Perhaps Jonathan could once again act as an intermediary, a peacemaker, between the two.

At this stage of his life the sturdy shepherd was very sensitive in spirit to the will and wishes of God. His long interludes of solitude with the sheep out on the range; his quiet communion with the Most High in the sanctuary of his own soul; even his private tutelage from God's prophet, Samuel, had fashioned a man of unusual forbearance and rare spiritual qualities.

His record so far, before both God and men, had been above reproach. He had experienced a meteoric career that commanded public attention, yet it was free of false-hood or deception. His name, now a household word throughout all of Israel, was held in the highest esteem. He was a hero to his people, not only for his daring exploits in the face of great danger, but also because of his noble character and impeccable conduct.

So in truth, and on very good grounds, he could demand of Jonathan: *"What have I done? What is mine iniquity? And what is my sin before thy father, that he seeketh my life?"* (1 Samuel 20:1).

This was not an exaggeration! It was a terse statement of truth. This was no time for theatrics between the two men. David's life was in jeopardy from Saul. This put a tremendous strain on both David and his friend.

For, in spite of his intense affection for David, Jonathan still felt a strong filial loyalty to his father. It was virtually a case of *"Blood runs thicker than the milk of human kindness."*

Jonathan tried to reassure David that he was certain no sinister evil would destroy him. Perhaps he somehow sensed with deep spiritual intuition that God's hand was upon his rugged friend to spare him for great future exploits. No matter what his father's demented designs, it seemed that Jonathan knew David would survive to supplant him.

It stands as a great credit to David that in spite of the terrible attacks from Saul, he did not seek revenge by driving a wedge between him and his son. Not once did David allow any desires he may have had to enjoy Jonathan's companionship in this crisis, to cause a family rift between father and son. He was wise enough to honor the integrity of Jonathan's home.

So staunch was David in his loyalty to both Saul and Jonathan that ultimately, even in their death, he could declare to all the world: *"Saul and Jonathan were lovely and pleasant in their lives, and in their death they were not divided!"* (2 Samuel 1:23).

It is a remarkable measure of David's generous spirit toward the royal family that he refused, even under the utmost provocation, to create a breech between them. Few men are this magnanimous. Most would have used their affection for the younger member to destroy the bonds of love between father and son.

But David would have none of this.

He had enormous respect for the sovereignty of Saul, even though he was a terrible tyrant.

He held the sanctity of this home and household in greater esteem than his own survival, for it was of God's own special appointment and anointing.

This was so true that David looked Jonathan full in the face and demanded that if he must die, now, at the hands of this family, it should be Jonathan's hands that did the dreadful deed.

The incredible and moving depths of their friendship is here seen in pulsing clarity. David is prepared to die, if need be, for the welfare of his friend. While Jonathan, for his part, is ready to risk his very life to determine what his father might do to destroy David.

Each was prepared to die for the other.

This is a clear reflection of the stirring love of God shed abroad in the spirits of both young stalwarts. It is a demonstration of that divine, supernatural love spoken of so often in the New Testament—a love that lays down its life for another.

Because of such sterling love between the two men, they could ventilate their most profound convictions without fracturing their friendship. Obviously there were strong differences of opinion. David was sure Saul was determined to destroy him. Subsequent events proved him right. Jonathan seemed equally convinced that his father, though a victim of passing evil moods, meant no permanent harm to David.

This seems strange, in light of Saul's repeated attempts to kill David, either in the privacy of his royal quarters, at Naioth or in his assignments against the Philistines.

At any rate David was determined to discover what Saul's true intentions were. So it was agreed that on the special feast day of the new moon he would absent himself from the royal table. If he were missed by the monarch, then Jonathan would plead his cause with the excuse that David had returned home to Bethlehem for a festive family reunion.

It seemed a small pivot point upon which a man's entire life would turn. But David was desperate at this point in his stormy career. He grasped at any straw in the wind that could give direction to his future.

The two men, being keen outdoorsmen, went out into a secluded spot in the nearby countryside. Here they would meet again three days later after Jonathan had sounded out Saul. But first they undertook to make solemn vows of lifelong loyalty to each other. They were entering into a compact of consummate allegiance to one another. No matter how violent or tragic events might become, their mutual friendship would never be sundered.

Jonathan loved David as he loved his own soul. He was determined that even if it meant they should never even see each other again, he would leave no stone unturned to warn his friend of impending peril. He was ready to forfeit the sweet consolation of his company to spare his life.

For Jonathan, with profound spiritual perception,

knew full well that he himself, though the first prince in Israel, would never ascend his father's throne. He was alert to the fact that David was God's chosen prince, anointed of Samuel years before to supplant him. Yet there was no ill will or rivalry in his heart.

Just as David respected Saul as God's anointed so likewise Jonathan regarded David as God's appointed king. He knew he would establish a new dynasty of rule in Israel. So a covenant was made between the two that out of honor for God's intentions, and integrity to each other, no harm would befall either family.

It was an unbreakable bond of astonishing generosity.

Even after Jonathan's untimely death, David honored his oath to his offspring.

As David had earlier suspected, Saul was angered by his absence from the banquet. When Jonathan was pressed about the matter he replied that his friend had begged leave of absence to visit his own family in Bethlehem.

Saul flew into a storm of fury. Typical of a schizophrenic, he raged against the imagined plot against himself. He was sure his son Jonathan would betray him. He was convinced that some dire scheme had been devised to usurp his throne.

In a wild outrage the unbalanced monarch heaped abuse on Jonathan. He slandered his mother, insulted his son and in the process behaved worse than any brute beast. Caught up in the terrifying toils of the dark spirit that seared his soul and scorched his spirit, Saul raved on like a maniac.

In a storm of ferocious frenzy he railed on against his son. The oaths and curses spilled from his quivering lips in a rush of verbal abuse. A black scowl creased his face which was flushed with anger. His eyes blazed with burning hate. His huge hulk trembled with the convulsion of his contempt.

Seizing a spear he flung it in fury at young Jonathan. The javelin would have skewered him to the wall, but he ducked from its flight. Now his own temper flamed white hot. No longer was he in doubt about his father's designs. He must warn David!

By a prearranged plan, Jonathan went out to the fields with a small lad. He took his bow and some arrows with him. Pulling it taut, his temper tightening his muscles, he shot the arrows far beyond the boy. It was the signal that all was not well at home. David would know for certain that there was no hope of his return to Saul's service.

The little lad was ordered to go in search of the arrows shot far over his head. As he did David came out of hiding. The lad, meanwhile, had been sent back to the city. He should not see the two princes fall into each other's arms. It was too tender, too precious, too moving a moment.

This was not a reunion!

It was in essence a parting of paths.

There was no place here now for further conversation. No time for more talk. No need for further discussion.

Both men, strong, upright, powerful warriors, fearless in combat, embraced fondly. Their affirmations of deep affection were punctuated with sobs of sorrow. This was the place of parting. Each, bound in unbreakable commitment to the other, would meet again only once.

They parted in peace. Jonathan would return to the royal city. David would go into permanent exile in the wilderness wastes. It was God's arrangement for them.

It was the Lord God Almighty who alone could preserve both men in peace until death did them part forever.

15
David at Nob

Up until this point in his remarkable young life David's reputation had been without reproach. His conduct both at home and in the king's court had been magnificent beyond his years. His record in battle had been heroic yet fierce as a falcon. He was a national hero who had won the hearts and favor of his generation.

The gracious Spirit of God, who rested upon him in such effulgence from the time of his special anointing under Samuel's hand, had imparted to David unusual wisdom and remarkable discretion. He moved surely, as one guided by God, whom he loved dearly and followed with complete trust.

His early psalms and songs written during this period of his career reflect this quiet confidence in the Most High. His years of solitude with his sheep; the quiet nights alone under the pulsing stars; his long, lonely days beneath the desert wind had given him ample opportunity to be still in soul, serene in spirit, before his God.

It was the spiritual legacy of his outdoor life and poignant times of intense communion with the Lord which enabled him to compose such exquisite poems as Psalms 8, 19 and 104. The very words ring with the majesty of the Almighty. *"What is man, that thou art mindful of him? And the son of man, that thou visitest him?"* (Psalm 8:4).

As has been well said, David was the sweet singer of Israel.

Then suddenly, upon parting with Jonathan, David's entire deportment took a violent turn of direction. It was as though the pain of separation from his dearest friend, the unrelenting fury of Saul, the isolation from his wife and family, combined to twist his soul and shrivel his normally buoyant spirit.

Instead of relying upon God for guidance as he had done before, David turned in upon himself, choosing rather to rely on his own human instincts for survival. It was a dreadful decision. The consequences would be so catastrophic that it would mean the painful death of innocent people as well as the defamation of his character. David's feet would be set on a downward trail of despair and destruction. His hands would become stained with the blood of terror and desolation.

To be fair to him we must see that at this point David felt enormous frustration. He had been separated from his closest friend. He had lost all favor with the king's court. He had been exiled from his wife and family associates. He was suddenly a desperado on the run. He who had been anointed to be king over his people was now more like a wild partridge hunted in the hills, taking flight to escape his foes.

For reasons not stated in the record, David felt his only recourse was to seek safety with the Philistines, his ancient enemy! He would seek asylum with Achish the king of Gath. In his flight he did not turn again to Samuel, but stopped instead to see the priest *Ahimelech* at *Nob.*

The name *Nob* means *"Nothing."* Evidently it was a nondescript spot where Ahimelech, an even less revered priest, was in residence. He was terrified when David turned up at his place all alone. Usually the young commanding officer was accompanied by a band of fighting men.

Somehow Ahimelech sensed something was wrong. He began to query David, but his questions were brushed aside. Instead, the fugitive, for the first time, resorted to outright deception. David insisted that the king had sent him on a secret mission—that this special assignment was strictly the king's business. He implied that it called for prompt action and daring disregard for any spiritual inhibitions that might stand in the way.

Of course all of these statements were essentially lies. They were flagrant falsehoods couched in language of duplicity and deception. The subtle art of saying one thing while meaning another is an ancient form of subterfuge. It has become a hallmark of our twentieth century society in the western world. Still it was an insidious method of double dealing in which David now indulged to gain personal advantage.

The supposed *"king"* on whose business he had come was not Saul at all. It was the synonym for David himself, who, having suddenly taken matters into his own hands, saw himself as *"king in his own castle."* Was he not anointed to be king? He would act as such!

Immediately David demanded that the hapless priest should provide him with provisions for his journey. The terrified Ahimelech protested weakly that he had no bread in hand except the sacred shewbread of the sanctuary.

David, in an uncharacteristic show of impatience,

swept aside the weak priest. He insisted that he be given
five of the small, hallowed loaves set aside for the service
of God. Ahimelech, in a divided mind, was hesitant to
let David have the sacred loaves lest he defile himself
and desecrate their use.

Again in a flagrant act of contempt for the spiritual
traditions of the priesthood David swept away all of
Ahimelech's objections. After all, he argued, both he
and his men, none of whom were with him, had not
been defiled for days. So why should there be any grounds
for withholding the bread from one going into battle?

As we contemplate the account, two things overwhelm
the senses. The first is David's contempt for the sacred
traditions of Israel's levitical ordinances. It is as if he suddenly deemed these of little consequence. He would bend
any law to meet his extremity. He would bludgeon any
person, even the priest, to meet his need. He would tell
any lie to achieve his goal.

Unfortunately both for David and the priest, Ahimelech capitulated to David's demands. Instead of standing
strong for the honor of God, he gave in to the young
warrior. Obviously Ahimelech was out of touch with God.
For, rather than turning David back to seek his strength
and confidence in the Lord, he simply added to his despair by granting him his unlawful desires. The pathetic
priest should have had enough spiritual courage to remind David of the great things Jehovah had done on
his behalf in the past. But he did not, and so he failed
miserably in his office.

Next David demanded weapons of war. It was a vivid
indication of how far he had turned from his trust in
the Most High. And why he should feel a priest could
supply him with a sword, shield and spear is difficult to
understand—the more so when it was he himself who
came against the giant Goliath without such armaments.

David had shouted in a ringing challenge for all the world to hear: *"You come against me with sword, shield and spear, but I come to you in the name of the Lord!"*

Again the tragic Ahimelech, knuckling under to David's demands, apologized that he had nothing in hand except the massive sword of Goliath. For some obscure reason the great, ungainly weapon was wrapped in a cloth and lay behind the priests' ephod. It really did not belong there. But still the weak-kneed priest dragged it out and handed it over to David.

The very sight of the shining steel aroused the blood in David's veins. *"Give it to me,"* he glowered.

Unfortunately for both David and Ahimelech, a man called Doeg, Saul's chief mule- and donkey-handler, stood in the shadows nearby and watched all that went on. He would report back to the king all the details of this dreadful day.

Unwittingly Ahimelech, by his cooperation with David, was sealing not only his own doom, but also that of his entire family. The out-working of his weak and hopeless compromise with David would destroy himself and lead David into the desert of spiritual degradation.

If Ahimelech had truly been God's spokesman he would have known David's duplicity. He would have stood against his wrong-doing. He would have turned him from his wicked ways. He would have reassured him of God's faithfulness and His capacity to succor him in this time of crisis.

But the priest did not do this. Entrusted with the spiritual leadership of his people, he failed both God and man. It is a most solemn warning to those who stand between God and men today. Like Ahimelech, many encourage their people to find their resources in the world and in its ways. When all the time they should be turning their people to God.

Unlike the fearless David of former times, the young warrior now fled in panic toward the coastal region of the Philistines. He was afraid of Saul, afraid of the future, afraid of his own web of falsehood that he was weaving around his own life, afraid even of the enemy, whom he once held only in contempt.

When David came to Gath, the Philistine stronghold where Achish was king, his arrival was greeted with utter disbelief. The enemy simply could not believe that this was Israel's most notorious and fabled warrior. Surely it was impossible that the fearless commanding officer of Israel's armed men should be at their city gates, a mere refugee.

In astonishment the Philistines refused to let him enter. Surely he was bent on mischief. He must have ulterior designs. Wasn't he the one who had slain Goliath? He was the one of whom the women sang, *"Saul has slain his thousands, but David his ten thousands!"*

In mortal terror for his life David decided on another strategy. He would surely perish at the hands of the very warriors he had routed in battle. Achish would have him slaughtered. There was only one escape. He must feign madness. It was known Saul was a mad man. Why not he?

With globs of saliva spilling down over his dark beard, David clawed and scrabbled with his fingers on the city gates. With garbled sounds and fiendish cries he tried to force his way into the city like one demented.

But Achish would have no part of his performance. The pagan king could see through the subterfuge. He had more spiritual perception than Ahimelech the priest.

As for David, it was one more dreadful, downward step into the darkness of his own self-degradation.

16
David, an Outlaw and Fugitive

In desperation, since Achish would not offer him asylum, David fled into the wilderness. There, like a hunted quarry, he took refuge in a remote rock cave. Its exact location has been disputed by scholars, but it may very well have been one of the desert hideouts not far from Bethlehem, with which David was familiar from his days as a shepherd.

Here amid the rough rock formations David felt the security of a sturdy outdoorsman who can survive by his wilderness skills. Here his untamed spirit was not shackled by the constricting niceties of civilization. David was really a rugged outlaw, banished by Saul, exiled now from the soft comforts of the king's court.

Word of his whereabouts quickly came to his family and relations not more than a few miles away. Out of concern and loving loyalty to him they soon joined the growing band of malcontents that began to gravitate to the young national hero. It was as if a strong and sinister underground movement was taking form in Israel. Many had become hostile to Saul.

Long before Saul had even been anointed king, the venerable old Samuel had warned the nation of this. He told them emphatically the new monarch would oppress them. Now his predictions had proved true. The result was a host of men who felt plundered, wronged and abused by Saul, now gathered as a rebel force around David. His wild fortress became the focal point of the nation's discontent.

It is a measure of David's unusual discretion that he decided his parents and near of kin should not be put in jeopardy because of him. So he made a swift cross-country excursion to Moab, east of the Dead Sea. This was the hot and formidable region from which his ancient maternal roots had come. Ruth, the remarkable Moabite widow, who married Boaz, was his great, great-grandmother.

In Moab David made arrangements for his aged parents to take refuge in comparative safety. At least they would escape any outrageous attacks Saul might try to make on them as retribution for David's actions. One never knew what mad and rash move the angry and unbalanced monarch might make.

David, meanwhile, now in hiding, longed to discern what future role he should play in God's plans for him. Though his own duplicity and deceit with Ahimelech had brought him down to this desperate point in his career, he still yearned for God's highest purposes. This remarkable aspect of his character, combined with a contrition of spirit that was ever ready to repent in humility of heart (will), endeared him to the Most High.

It was amid the darkness and desperation of the cave of Adullam that David composed Psalms 34 and 56: *"The Lord is nigh unto them that are of a broken heart; and saveth such as be of a contrite spirit. Many are the afflictions of the righteous; but the Lord delivereth him out of them all"* (Psalm 34:18–19).

Such truths have stirred the souls and quickened the spirits of God's people for well over 3,000 years. They have been the cry of confidence for the oppressed from generation to generation, whether under the tyranny of Saul, or the iron heel of twentieth-century dictators.

Amid his grief, amid his exile, amid his rebel comrades David was learning first hand the frustration and anguish of the oppressed. He would develop an enormous empathy for the underprivileged of his people. Never would he be immune to the suffering of his subjects when in due time he became their monarch.

In the caves, the wildest hideouts and desert wastes of a fierce and hostile region, David was binding the hearts of his comrades to him with strands of steel-like love and loyalty. No king had ever before tasted the bitter fruit of utter alienation as he did now. No monarch would endure such humiliation, abuse and degradation at the cruel whims of his oppressor.

Because of all this in due course he would become the most beloved ruler ever to reign in Israel, for he knew fully what it was to be the underdog in society. He had been among the poorest of the poor. He had literally tasted the very pangs of death as his life stood ever in peril.

We do well to remind ourselves that in the fullness of time another, greater than David, monarch of the universe, Christ the Anointed, suffered in the same manner for all of us.

Saul, meanwhile, had returned to his home village of Gibeah. There in the cool shade of the feathery tamarisk trees he held court from day to day. It was a typical scene with the local people hovering around listening to the pompous personage regale his audience with political propaganda.

The arrogant tyrant was in an expansive mood. Word had come to him that David had been discovered. He was now in hiding in the forest of Hareth. Here he could soon be brought to bay. It would be much easier than trying to take him in his rocky fortress.

It had been a bold step of strong faith and quiet obedience for David to leave his cave of security and go to Hareth. But that had been God's clear command to him through the prophet Gad. Because of his prompt compliance with the will of God his life would be spared, as well as those of his men.

Others less fortunate would fall under the mad fury of Saul's cruel, avenging temper. Even innocent men, women and children would be annihilated in his bitter anger.

Day after day Saul harangued his hearers. Spear in hand, he strutted his stuff, giving vent to the angry emotions that boiled up within his being. He was sure all of Israel was set against him. He roared that his contemporaries had conspired with David to overthrow him. He bellowed like a bull, enraged that even his son Jonathan was a traitor to him.

He challenged the nondescript crowd that came to hear him: *"Will David give everyone of you fields, vineyards and special commissions in the army?"* (see 1 Samuel 22:7). Could the son of Jesse ever make up to them what he himself had taken from them? The convoluted thinking of his deranged mind was a tortured tirade against even his own associates. Saul seemed to see in everyone a potential enemy. He felt even his closest friends and family members were traitors who had betrayed his trust.

Letting his imagination run riot he accused them all of subterfuge. They were making dastardly schemes to destroy him. He was sure every man's sword was set against him. In sickening self-pity and wretched, blind, jealous rage he ranted on against his subordinates.

Precisely at this point the crafty Doeg stepped forward from the mob. It was the opportunity he had waited for to ingratiate himself with the tyrant. They were two of a kind, both ruthless, warped men. It was more than just their common love of donkeys that had drawn them to each other. Their twisted, hostile spirits found mutual attraction in one another, like springs of tempered metal intertwined.

Doeg, with gloating words and smoldering eyes, recounted to Saul how he had stood in the shadows watching the priest Ahimelech, aiding and abetting David. He had sought the counsel of God for the young fugitive. He had given him bread for strength, Goliath's sword for battle.

In burning fury Saul commanded that the priest, and all his family, as well as the other lesser priests at Nob, be summoned into his presence at once. He would not brook a moment's delay. He himself would question Ahimelech's outrageous conduct.

When they came, Saul, beside himself with rage, demanded to know why the priest had aided David. Ahimelech replied without rancor or disrespect. He simply insisted that David was due all the courtesy extended to him.

After all, wasn't David the commanding officer in Israel's army? Wasn't he the one, who, above all others had been faithful in serving both the nation and Saul? Wasn't he the one who had conducted himself with such dignity in Saul's court? Wasn't he Saul's own son-in-law, married to his own daughter?

Surely such a noble person in the nation was deserving of his service! He had only done his duty!

Ahimelech's reply only added fuel to the flames of Saul's fury. Leaping to his feet—towering like a smoldering inferno over the unfortunate priests—the mad monarch roared, *"Ahimelech, you and all your father's family will surely die for this!"*

He turned to the armed guards who stood around him and commanded them to kill the priests. They refused to obey. They would not lift their hands against the Lord's anointed servants. What courage!

Not to be deterred, Saul turned to his head donkey driver, Doeg. *"You do the dirty work!"* Without a second thought Doeg, the pagan Edomite, drew his sword and slaughtered the helpless priests.

In cold blood, without a tinge of remorse, the cruel Canaanite hacked and butchered eighty-five men to death before the blood-thirsty Saul. Unarmed, clad only in their priestly robes, the victims of such outrageous violence went down like dry weeds cut by a scythe. Blood ran across the ground, soaked the soil and seared the crass conscience of the king.

He was not done!

The next day Doeg would destroy every remaining vestige of life at Nob. Men, women, servants, children, infants, livestock, all would be wiped out. Nob literally became "nothing." Saul, who deliberately refused to obey God and do this to Amalek, had not hesitated to do it to this special household of the Most High. Such was his utter perverseness of spirit.

Only one priest escaped the terrible assassination. It

124

was young Abiathar who fled to David and recounted the carnage. David was man enough to realize that the root cause of the catastrophe had been his own deception.

Without excuse or flimflam he bore the blame for the dreadful bloodbath. No man lives to himself. The consequences of our actions go on to fulfillment.

David's only remaining consolation to Abiathar was, *"Abide with me: fear not . . . thou shalt be in safeguard"* (1 Samuel 22:23). What faith!

17

David Betrayed by Those He Helps

News of the deep rift between King Saul and David swept across the country. It was as if the first dark, ominous shadows of a civil war were being cast over Israel by the horrible slaughter of the innocent priests at Nob.

The cruel atrocities committed under Saul's orders, though carried out by Doeg, had been the direct result of David's deception of Ahimelech. The latter had failed God in his priestly office by not turning the desperate David from the wicked ways upon which his feet were set.

Word of the calamity quickly reached even into the enemy camps of the Philistines. Quick to take advantage of the situation, they launched a raid of attrition against Keilah, a small frontier community on the southwest borders of Israel. Their main objective was to gather up the newly harvested grain crop from the threshing floors.

It was a typical enemy maneuver. Whenever God's people are divided and caught up in conflict over any issue, be it spiritual or secular, the enemy moves in to exploit the controversy. He will hamper the harvest and raid the strongholds of those loyal to the Lord.

The news of the Philistines plundering Keilah aroused David. Immediately he inquired of the Most High if he should save Keilah. The reply was positive. So David was eager for battle.

But his ragtag band of followers were much less so. The nondescript group of malcontents who had gathered around David were not the boldest of men at this point. They admitted freely that even as fugitives in Judah, they lived in mortal terror of their lives. They were hardly a fit fighting force to take on the Philistines.

Again David sought counsel of the Lord. A second time he was assured he should attack. God's word to him was that he would triumph under the mighty hand of God's deliverance.

With renewed faith in the Almighty, not in himself, David ignored the fear of his followers and led them into action. It was a tremendous rout of the enemy. The city was spared, and David's men came away with enormous booty of cattle, spoils of war and battle gear that would sustain them in future engagements.

Without realizing it, the armed fugitives were being shaped into a formidable underground force. Even though the young priest Abiathar joined David in this attack at Keilah, in essence David and his men were being welded into a terrorist band whose later atrocities would equal those Saul committed at Nob.

It was for fear that a similar dreadful outrage might be perpetrated against them that the people of Keilah not only alerted the king that David was there, but even offered to deliver him up to Saul as a hostage. The youthful commander was not to be that easily trapped.

To us it seems incongruous that a community spared from enemy depredation would be so callous. It is the essence of ingratitude to betray one's benefactor. But David lived in tough times among a cruel and cunning people. Most of them sought only their own self interests.

David, in humility of spirit, twice entreated Abiathar the priest to determine God's wishes for him. Should he stay in Keilah and face Saul's wrath there? Or should he flee again as a fugitive? Even though he had done only good, it was made clear to him he would be destroyed if he remained.

With clear guidance from God, the raider quietly slipped out of the town with his men. They would disappear into the desert wastes where their ancient skills as tough outdoorsmen would preserve them from Saul's army in hot pursuit.

It is noteworthy that David made no attempt to avenge himself on Keilah for its gross ingratitude. Lesser men might have plundered the town in a towering rage. Or they might have set fire to its homes. They might even have slaughtered some of the men and ravished their women.

But David did none of these. His forbearance for his own people is most impressive. It stands as a premiere example of the patience and longsuffering God looks for in His people.

Most of us find it infuriating when those we benefit fail to appreciate our help. In our modern society ingratitude becomes increasingly common.

Christians are often deeply troubled by this. They need not be. Christ, when He was here, often endured the same sort of abuse. His counsel to us is clear and precise . . . *"Love ye your enemies, and do good, and lend (help), hoping for nothing again; and your reward shall be great, and ye shall be children of the Highest: for he is kind unto the unthankful, and to the evil. Be ye therefore merciful, as your Father also is merciful"* (Luke 6:35–36).

Our God is not only the God of all mercy, consolation

and comfort. He is also the God of all compensation to His people. It is He who in wondrous ways and with stunning surprises, which I call "His beautiful bonuses," makes up to us any losses we may suffer in well-doing.

It is considered clever in contemporary society to ridicule and belittle those who do good. The cynics and skeptics of our day abuse those who would live like the Master. Let it never deter us from doing noble service. Let it never keep us from pleasing God. Let it never discourage us from living lofty lives as God's men and women.

David did not! God saw it and was pleased. And the consequence was that a beautiful bonus came to the young fugitive in his wilderness hideout. For, all of a sudden, one day, amid his solitude and loneliness Jonathan showed up.

The two stalwarts must have literally fallen into each other's embrace. The long separation had only made their hearts grow fonder. The reunion was charged with emotion.

It was at tremendous risk to himself that the gallant prince Jonathan went into the wilderness to find his friend. Had Saul known about it he would surely have slaughtered his son in wild abandon. Despite such dangers Jonathan was deeply constrained to encourage David in the Lord. He did not hesitate to put his own life in jeopardy to fortify the faith of his friend.

Jonathan reassured David that in due course he would become king over the nation. He held firm the hope that he himself might be next in command to him. Once more they renewed their lifelong covenant of loyalty and fidelity to one another.

Two strong, virile fighting men, lithe as leopards, swift as desert falcons, stood facing each other for the last time and swore utter allegiance before God and men. Over their heads stretched the vast expanse of the night sky, studded with stars. Around their powerful figures flowed the dry hot wind of the desert wastes. A small campfire crackled at their feet, its flames throwing their rugged features into bold relief.

Neither of them knew it, but they would never, ever meet again. This was their final parting. Only the strong wind of God's own gracious Spirit would or could traverse the great distances between the two, binding and uniting their spirits as one.

Jonathan had achieved the loftiest service any man can attain in life. He had strengthened his friend's faith in God.

It would be God who would preserve David in his perilous career. It would be God who would deliver him again and again from the tyranny of Saul. It would be God who would raise him up from exile to become the greatest monarch Israel ever knew.

Having heard that David had slipped out of Keilah, Saul called off his planned siege of the city. But not long after word was sent to him from the people of Ziph that the fugitive and his followers were now hiding out in the rugged terrain south of them.

This region had long been known as one of the most remote and hostile areas in the country. Its deep dongas, dry wadis and rough rock formations made it possible for terrorists to find refuge in the broken desert landscape. Only the local residents around Jeshimon would ever be able to track down those who lurked in this formidable region.

Saul was elated when reports reached him that the people of Ziph would give him support in his search for David. He was convinced this was a clear omen from God that he had found some loyal citizens who had compassion for him as a person and would support his cruel cause.

Little did the demented king realize how wrong he was. Again and again, instead of seeking the mind of God, in his own stubborn self-assertion he had done just the opposite. He had grieved God's Spirit by his own way-wardness. He had sealed his own certain self-destruction by his vicious hatred against one innocent man!

In fury Saul launched a major expedition into the desert wasteland. He came almost within arrow shot of capturing David when suddenly a dispatch came telling of another major attack by the Philistines. The enemy had invaded the land. There remained no choice but to turn back from pursuing David, who escaped by a hair's breadth.

From here David fled even deeper into the hot wasteland known as *Engedi*. This was a region famous for its tiny secretive water seeps where the wild and beautiful *ibex* came to slake their thirst.

Only God's intervention in bringing in the Philistine invaders had spared David from certain death. But such divine help came to David, not because he was a faultless man (he was far from it), but because he was a man who above all else wished to do God's will.

David had gradually been forged into a tough and ruthless terrorist himself, just to survive. And though it is thought that he composed Psalms 31 and 54 during this difficult and formidable period in the desert wastes, he was not just "Israel's Sweet Singer."

As later events would demonstrate, David was becoming a desperado. His tactics would put terror into many lives. The blood of whole communities would be spilled by his hands. He would become a ruthless raider. Yet the wonder of it all was that out of such depths he would be lifted up by the Lord to be called *"a man after God's own heart"*—one who above all else desired to do God's will.

18
The Ruined Robe

The new Philistine invasion of Israel served only as a temporary diversion from Saul's relentless pursuit of his archrival. The angry monarch was consumed with jealousy and contempt for David. His hostility, it seemed, would and could only be appeased by the death of the younger man.

In his madness Saul gathered up a force of 3,000 fully armed men to search for the fugitive. Word had reached Saul that David had withdrawn into the desolate wasteland of the Ibex Springs. It was a region as tough and formidable as the Kofa Wildlife Refuge of southern Arizona. Burned by scorching heat, where the sun flames like a searing torch, it was a hostile spot to hunt a man in hot blood.

Here there were some ancient sheep pens, fashioned from rocks in the tumbled terrain. Saul guessed David's shepherd instincts might draw him to the area. And he was right. David and his little handful of men had holed up in the sheltering darkness of the rough rock caves that honeycombed the country.

In an incredible turn of events the king chose to enter the very cave in which his rival was ensconced. Some scholars believe that in common with many royal personages Saul suffered from severe constipation—*"the curse of kings."* There alone in the seclusion of the cave Saul struggled to relieve himself. Little did he know that he was almost within arm's length of the very man he sought. Apparently he was so preoccupied he did not even hear the whispers of the armed warriors in the darkness.

Excited at the chance given to David to destroy his antagonist, his companions urged him to take revenge. *"This is the day the Lord has placed your angry opponent in your power!"* they whispered to him in hushed voices. *"Do what you wish!"* (see v. 4).

It was a tense moment. The temptation to sever Saul's head from his neck with one swift stroke of Goliath's sword must have burned in David's emotions. It would be so easy, so sudden, so sure! But somehow he would not, could not, raise his powerful arm against God's anointed, chosen king.

Instead David slipped up behind the monarch, and with a swift, sharp stroke of his sword severed the long train from the royal robe. It was an act of utter contempt for the one who wore it. It was a gesture of degradation. It was a total humiliation more potent than could be put in human language.

This was an expression of the utmost disdain and disrespect David could show Saul. In a single stroke of his alien sword David had disclosed his dark, inner hatred. The blackness of his heart's hostility was matched by the pervading darkness of this dark and dusty cave. He despised the Lord's anointed. And, though he had not murdered the tyrant in cold blood, he had in fact shown that he murdered him in his heart.

For David it was a moment of truth.

Suddenly there flashed upon his conscience an acute awareness of his awful attitude toward Saul.

He was in the white light of God's presence in that place. He had plunged to the same depths of degradation as his opponent. He was stricken with remorse at the intense hostility of his heart. His sinister, dark outrage brought him down to the dust of self-reproach.

In the intensity of his revulsion against his wrong behavior, David touched the keystone of true repentance. Saul may have been grunting and groaning in physical discomfort amid the gloom of that dusty cave. But David was groaning in spirit with the agony of a soul that sees itself stripped and laid bare of all false pretense.

In bold defiance of the angry warriors around him, David apologized for his rash behavior. How dare he vent his hostility against his superior in this crude gesture? How dare he despise God's anointed person with such disgusting disgrace?

Nor would he allow one of his "young lions" to touch a hair of Saul's handsome head. Not one would run a shining spear through his cruel heart.

Unscathed, Saul stood up, adjusted his royal robe and strode out of the darkness into the blinding desert sunlight. He did not know it, but he looked as absurd as a newly clipped poodle, shorn of its long and handsome coat.

He had gone only a few yards when the shout of a man's voice arrested him. Turning swiftly he saw a warrior, face to the ground, bowing in the dust before him.

The hunched figure of the fully armed man, crouched at the cave's mouth, began to speak. The sounds of his voice, somewhat muffled, came clearly enough that Saul soon recognized that it was none other than David. Terrified, awestruck, almost beyond belief that his life had been spared, Saul stood rooted to the ground unable to run, move or speak.

In an outpouring of emotion David gave vent to the surging tide of intense inner conflict of soul surging through him. In one instant he claimed absolute innocence. He insisted that he meant no harm against Saul. He protested that despite the prompting of his fellow warriors he refused to do the dreadful deed of slaying him.

He had been given every chance to even the score. He had been accused often of scheming to destroy the king, when in fact he was not so minded. Here was irrefutable evidence of those false charges, for he had let Saul go free. How dare he raise his sword to shed the royal blood of the Lord's anointed?

Yet in the next instant David, torn by his own inner anguish of spirit, flung up his arm to display the long train of Saul's royal robe. It fluttered in the hot wind, one end cut all askew by the razor-sharp edge of Goliath's sword. Here was the ultimate insult. Here was proof positive that only the restraining power of God's Spirit had kept him from plunging that shining steel into Saul's warm flesh.

For David, the tumble of wild words that came from his hot lips and hot heart, was an outpouring of contrite confession before both God and man. In one breath he claimed innocence. In the next he admitted his evil inner attitude.

This dichotomy is not something strange to the sons and daughters of men. All of us have known all too well the fierce inner conflicts of our convoluted souls. Just because we do not take actual revenge into our own hands we protest our pure innocence. Yet at the same time we are consumed by bitterness, rancor and burning animosity against our antagonist who has wronged us.

We say we are without fault, while all the time we know full well we are wrong.

The Word of God addresses this matter very clearly: *"Whosoever hateth his brother is a murderer"* (1 John 3:15).

It is only the frank and open admission of our guilt that can allow the free flowing forgiveness of the life of God to cleanse our conscience of its evil. This David was doing. From this he did not shrink back. Though he was a fierce and formidable fighting man, David's spirit was one which could be contrite before the Lord and honestly humble before his enemies. It was his redeeming grace.

Unashamedly he shouted to Saul, *"My hand shall not hurt you. It must be God who arbitrates between us. I will do you no harm, though you hunt me like a dog"* (see v. 12).

This was the cry of a truly converted soul!

The transforming light of God's Spirit had shone into David's anguished soul in that dark cave. It exceeded in brightness the searing desert sun outside. He saw, as Paul saw on the Damascus road, that his hate had been directed not just against a man, but against God Himself who yearned over the life of that man.

As for Saul, the sound of David's familiar voice, so clear, so strong, so appealing, touched the well-spring of his unstable emotions. He burst into hot tears, the scalding drops cascading down his flushed face. Terror and relief engulfed him in the same measure. He had been in the very grip of death, yet was mercifully spared.

"You are more righteous than I," he called out in his extremity. *"You have rewarded me good, whereas I have rewarded you evil!"* (see v. 17). He threw up his great

139

sinewy arms in the ancient gesture of good will. *"You have dealt with me in generosity, when you could have killed me! The Lord reward you with his blessings for your mercy to me!"* (see vv. 16–19).

For Saul, this, too, was a moment of truth.

It might well have been the pivotal point of his life. It could have been the great divide at which he turned away from walking in his wickedness. The intense illumination which flooded into his darkened soul to reveal his own inner perversion should have been his conversion. But it was not!

His mind had been touched and made rational.
His emotions had been stirred to see his sin.
But his stubborn will, (his hard heart), remained set, bolted, sealed and barred against God.

What was true for Saul on that cataclysmic day, at the mouth of the cave, is true today for uncounted thousands of so-called Christians—carnal Christians. With their minds they realize the reasonableness of Christ's claim on their lives. They even give mental assent to their condition of character. In their emotions they may have been overwhelmed with the awareness of their inner wrongs. Floods of tears may have been shed for their sins.

But because the central citadel of their wills has never been breached by the convicting presence of God's own Spirit, no permanent change occurs in their lives. Their characters are not altered. Their old, selfish, evil ways persist. There is no true conversion—no true turning to God, asking Him to control the life.

This was painfully obvious in Saul. Before parting from David he had the colossal audacity to extract a covenant promise from him that he would spare his progeny and protect his posterity when he came to power.

140

Like Jonathan, Saul knew full well David would supplant him. He was completely aware this was God's arrangement. Yet deep in his twisted, tormented spirit he was determined to short-cut the divine destiny of young David. He would destroy him!

David was astute enough to see through Saul's sham. Though the monarch went home, David chose to remain in his wilderness stronghold.

19
David and Nabal

Thirty-three years of Saul's tyranny had burdened Israel when Samuel, old and weary with the wrongs of his people, died. He had been the last of the judges to guide Israel under God. In his own right, he had been a prophet without reproach before the Most High. He had lived under the cloud of Saul's intransigence, yet he did so with dignity.

So the entire nation mourned his passing with profound emotion. It was he who had warned them of the disasters that would come upon them in establishing a human monarchy. Only his keen sensitivity to God's Spirit in choosing another king (David) could spare God's people from annihilation at the hands of their ancient foes.

Now, without his venerable presence in Israel, the nation faced the prospect of even further cleavage between Saul and David. For in due course a deep rift would develop between the tribe of Judah from which David came and the rest of the nation, to be known as Israel.

In the meantime David and his men, now about 600 in number, moved westward from the southern deserts.

He was in search of supplies to sustain his followers. Surviving in the heat and draught of the Negev was a tough ordeal.

As they approached the rugged sheep ranges of Paran and Maon, David heard that a prosperous sheepman named Nabal was shearing his flock in Carmel.

This Carmel is not the same mountain promontory on the coast where Elijah would later slay the prophets of Baal. Rather it was the upper desert region given to Caleb as a special inheritance by Joshua, when Israel occupied Canaan.

Sheep-shearing is always done during the hottest time of the year. Next to lambing time, it is the most difficult period of labor. The shearing crews, stripped to the waist, with sweat streaming off them, manhandle the sheep with brute strength and great skill.

Sheep do not relish being sheared. They struggle and kick and stiffen their necks in fear of the shears that slide and glide swiftly between fleece and pelt. The wool is foul with dust, burs, ticks, dung and other debris. In the heat the lanolin and other sheep odors are pungent and repulsive.

So the job is always rushed. The ewes and lambs are corralled for as short a time as possible, lest they lose weight and condition. Everything demands strength, energy and drive to get done. Men's tempers flare easily and anger is ignited by the least interruption.

David, having been a shepherd himself, knew all this. He was completely familiar with the tensions and strains of shearing time—the more so when thousands of sheep had to be clipped. Surely he was wise enough to recall that this was an interlude in which one did not intrude on a sheepman's operations.

But apparently he chose to do so anyway. Why, it is hard to say.

144

He sent off a band of ten young men to see Nabal. They were to report that it was David who sent them, with his personal regards. They were to remind Nabal that his herders and flocks had been given protection and courtesy whenever they were encountered in the desert. Lastly he requested that the wealthy operator be generous enough to supply him with provisions for his men.

On the surface all of this might appear legitimate. But to a rough and surly individual like Nabal it was not. Livestock men are a tough breed. They must be to survive. Too often they are misrepresented as sweet, gentle characters who love animals and everyone else.

Not so! Witness the violent range wars that raged across the western United States between stock owners for years.

Nabal was no exception. He was furious because David's men interrupted his work. He was incensed to think the desert fugitive would demand supplies from him, simply because he had not raided the flocks in the field. What right did he have to them anyway? And lastly, why should David and his men celebrate at his expense, when he and his crews were working themselves to the bone?

In hot anger he heaped insults on David, growling in disdain, *"Who is David? Who is the son of Jesse? Who is this one who breaks away from his master?"* (see 1 Samuel 25:10).

It was the ultimate insult—a most unwise move! Just as for David, sending his men at this time, was a most rash and thoughtless action.

Both men were deeply at fault.

Both of them now had their blood up.

Both of them were consumed with rage.

There is a most important principle at work here. It is that spiritual discretion stated so clearly in Ecclesiastes

3: *"There is a time to every purpose under the heaven. . . . a time to keep silence, and a time to speak. A time to love, and a time to hate, a time of war, and a time of peace"* (see 3:1–8).

Few of God's people ever fully understand or master this concept. It is the essence of wisdom. It is the sure formula for good will. It is one of the supreme secrets to success in human relationships.

David, in his lack of understanding and hot-headed impetuosity, determined he would wipe out not only Nabal but all his kinsmen as well.

In violent outrage at Nabal's insults he ordered 400 of his men to arm themselves at once. He himself, with eyes blazing and adrenalin pouring into his blood stream, would go up against this arrogant sheepman and annihilate the entire male population.

For David this was a dangerous drift in the direction of violence. Its first faltering step was when he came within a hair's breadth of beheading Saul in the cave. Even though he settled for lopping off the king's royal robe, his conscience had smitten him in anguish.

Yet here again, so soon, he was on the point of taking another man's life in the heat of his own anger and hot blood.

The deep repentance and profound remorse of his encounter with Saul seems to have been swept away in the floodtide of his furious emotions. He had not yet come to that point in his walk with God where his feelings had come under the control of God's Spirit.

But for the mercy and intervention of the Most High, David, at this juncture in his career, might well have done both Nabal and himself irreparable damage. But God did intervene—He did send someone to turn David aside from the desperation of the moment.

David and Nabal

This was not the first time God had proved faithful to the fearsome young warrior. The reader will recall that in the rock hideout of Adullam, the prophet Gad was sent to urge David to leave. At Keilah young Abiathar the priest was sent to direct David's actions. In the wilderness of Ziph his friend Jonathan had been inspired to come and encourage his comrade.

And now once more, David is spared from great evil, for on his way to massacre Nabal, he meets the man's wife, Abigail. She is an astonishing woman, not only singularly beautiful in appearance, but also of winsome personality and enormous wisdom.

Word had come to her that David's men had approached her husband for help. She had also been told that they had been treated very badly by her churlish mate. Moreover, she had been warned that because of the insults and abuse heaped on David he was bound to take terrible revenge on her husband.

Abigail was wise enough to know that only her personal intervention could possibly defuse this explosive confrontation. Quickly she ordered her servants to gather up some supplies which would serve as a peace offering to the desert fugitive.

Loading these on donkeys, she and her personal attendants set out to meet the angry invader. Seeing him in the distance she dismounted and prostrated herself before David in the dust.

It was a most daring action, for in the culture of those times a woman bore no noble standing in society. Most men would not even touch food or drink from the hand of a strange woman. Even if a woman's shadow were to fall across a man's meal it was considered defiled and unfit to eat.

So it called for remarkable generosity of the hostile

young warrior even to give Abigail his attention. Most men in such a mood would simply have passed her by with a sneer of contempt. Yet here now, in his moment of peril, David had sufficient spiritual perception to see that this brave lady was a messenger from the Lord.

In an outpouring of profound humility Abigail apologized for her husband's brutal behavior. She was greathearted enough to assume part of the blame herself. And in contrition she pled for David to realize that he was ordained of God for great service to his people.

Her earnest eloquence diffused David's anger. It quieted the surging hostility of his spirit.

Looking down upon her bowed form he replied softly. *"Blessed be God who sent you to meet me this day. Blessed be your wise advice, and you yourself, for keeping me from shedding blood and avenging myself with my own hand. . . . Go in peace! . . . I have heard your voice and accepted your person!"* (see v. 32 ff.).

It was a remarkable concession for David to make. It set her mind at rest, her emotions at peace. In quiet repose she turned around and returned home.

There a tremendous banquet was under way. The hot and smelly shearing was over for another year. The wretched work was all behind them. So Nabal threw a fabulous feast for all his men. The wine ran red, so that everyone became thoroughly intoxicated.

Abigail, with her keen perception, knew this was no time to tell Nabal about her encounter with David. Astute and wise lady that she was, she waited until the next day to break the news to her husband. When the wine had gone out of him she reported how his life had hung as by a single strand of raw wool. David and his warriors would surely have wiped him out along with all his kinsmen, had she not acted.

Nabal was stunned!

It was as if he had been struck with a bolt from the blue.

Suddenly he was gripped with a horrendous heart seizure. His will to live was broken. His fierce anger faded.

Ten days later he was dead.

David quietly bowed his head, humbled by the vengeance of God upon his adversary.

20
David and Abigail

The initial encounter between Abigail and David made such a stunning impact upon David that he immediately proposed marriage to her after the sudden death of Nabal. Her prompt acceptance indicated that she, in turn, had been equally impressed with him.

It was no small thing to be wed to a man who was a fugitive. Even though David was the most highly esteemed fighting man in Israel, for years to come he would live as an exile away from his own people. Abigail's life would not be easy or comfortable. For she, too, like her husband would have to live in dire danger as a member of the underground.

Unlike Michal, David's first bride, who opted for the pleasures and comforts of the king's court, this woman was ready to follow her daring David into the desert wastes. Michal, like her father Saul, preferred to break her fidelity to her husband rather than remain true to him in his wanderings as a desert brigand.

So the two women were direct opposites in character. In fact, Michal actually allowed her cruel father to use her as a source of sorrow to David when she was given in marriage to another man. Of course, David may have considered himself fortunate to be rid of a wife like Michal. But the record left to us does not say so, and later events indicate otherwise.

After all, he and his companions had gone to great risk to kill 200 Philistines to win her hand. The woman Abigail would now take Michal's place. So she deserves our careful scrutiny.

The name Abigail means "one of good understanding." Obviously she was much more than merely intelligent. The biblical description implies the idea of a person with a profound capacity to grasp spiritual values. Abigail had an intimate knowledge of the living God. She was not just a sharp lady—she was also a gracious woman whose conduct was controlled by the Spirit of the Lord.

Probably her marriage to such a tragic individual as Nabal had been one of those arranged affairs characteristic of her culture. It was not a matter of personal choice. So like multitudes of women she was placed in a difficult dilemma, living with a man who was not only sullen and morose, but quite obviously antagonistic to God.

The term "son of Belial" used to describe Nabal, is an ancient term for one who turns away from Jehovah to serve false gods. The apparent success and prosperity he enjoyed in accumulating large numbers of sheep and goats must have been due in some measure to this magnificent woman to whom he was married.

Her keen mind, enormous tact, sweet spirit, attractive appearance and deep devotion to God had brought strength and stability into the marriage. And even though Nabal, as his name *"folly"* implies, lacked the capacity for success, their prosperity had come nonetheless simply because of this gracious woman.

She epitomizes the highest and finest qualities to be found among women. She represents that generous, loving, self-giving attribute which so often sets women apart from men.

Despite all the clamor of modern society to equate men and women, the fact remains they are not the same. There is inherently deep within the feminine disposition an element of concern, generosity, selflessness and love that gives and gives and gives. This dimension of life is in large measure lacking in men.

Were it made up only of men, the world would be an awful place of brutality and selfish aggression. It would be stripped of much that is noble, lovely and tender if the presence of wonderful women was lacking. The women of the world so often bring the touch of kindness, the compassion of caring, the healing of generosity, the graciousness of self-giving into a hard and brash society.

And it is the great tragedy of the twentieth century that women's liberation movements would deceive women into believing they should behave like men. It is an awesome loss to all of us. In so doing women lose their greatest gift, their charm, their loveliness, their winsome warmth of love. Their children lose their mothers, with the deep understanding and loving compassion godly mothers can provide. Men lose the faithful loyalty and deep devotion of true lifemates who can make them stand ten feet tall, brave to face any challenge that comes.

Abigail was all woman in the finest sense of the word.

The moment word came to her of Nabal's insult to David and his men, she knew she had to act to save everyone involved. Not only was she concerned for her own family, but also she was alarmed for the great evil David would bring on himself by such violent bloodshed.

Noble woman that she was, she did not turn on Nabal,

berating him for his belligerence. Nor did she heap abuse on the man for his incredible folly.

He had done a most stupid thing in arousing David's anger. Both were "macho" men. They were inflamed with pride; their tempers burned. Hostility was ignited between them. And she was caught in the middle.

But Abigail did not berate her husband for his folly. Nor did she turn to tears for release. Neither did she succumb to self-pity and fear for her family. Instead she took brave, bold steps to mend the breach between the two antagonists. In courageous self-sacrifice she was prepared to literally fling herself into the gap to bring peace where violence was emerging.

Risking the ferocious temper of Nabal, she promptly commandeered food supplies from the stores set aside for his shearers. She loaded 200 loaves of bread, two huge containers of wine, five sheep carcasses, five large containers of corn, 200 cakes of figs and 100 clusters of raisins on a small band of donkeys. Then, mounting her own ass, she rode off gallantly to meet David and his armed men.

She was on a mission of mercy, determined to spare her own menfolk as well as preserve David's dignity. She left without fanfare. Not even Nabal knew she was gone. Love was stealing away softly to do its own noble deeds. The risks were enormous for her as a woman, for no female approached a strange man without invitation. To do so was to court disaster and rejection.

Like Queen Esther of a later era, Abigail knew full well that to make this move was literally to lay her own life on the line. In effect she was saying, *"If I perish, I perish"* (see Esther 4:16). One word of command from the desert warrior and her life could have been wiped out as swiftly as the flash of a sword.

154

Abigail met the approaching mob of armed men in a deep defile, perhaps a dry wadi burning with desert heat. She must have been fully veiled against the hot sun and from the probing eyes of the fierce men searching her features.

In an act of humble obeisance she slipped smoothly from her saddle, prostrating herself in the hot dust as David rode up to her. She flung herself upon the warrior's mercy in total self-abandonment.

"Upon me, my lord, upon me let this iniquity be" (v. 24). Her voice was low, soft, well-modulated, utterly sincere. *"Let thine handmaid, I pray thee, speak in thine audience."* She paused a brief moment. *"O, hear the words of thine handmaid!"* (v. 24).

David must have made some gesture to indicate she would be given a hearing. Her courage, her humility, her selflessness, her self-composure arrested his attention. She could not be ignored!

Then there tumbled from her lips words of calm entreaty that could flow only from a heart of compassion—a spirit overflowing with love and an intellect of remarkable astuteness.

Using gentle tact she begged David to overlook and disregard her husband's folly. Surely he could understand that Nabal in his estrangement from God would not, could not, show the necessary respect for the Lord's anointed. If David's men had come to her, instead of her husband, things would have been different.

To make amends she was bringing a peace offering of provisions for David. It would be a token of her esteem. And it would be a blessing to him. It would help to defuse his anger and turn away his wrath.

In a bold gesture of enormous confidence, yet quiet faith in the Most High, she assured David it was the mercy of God that would restrain him from murdering all her menfolk. To her great credit she did not rant or rave against this brigand bent on bloodshed. Instead she appealed to his deepest spiritual springs.

She had encountered David at one of the low points in his life. His emotions burned white hot, out of control. His pride flamed in maddened fury against her family. His heart was black with hate, so that there engulfed his entire being the attitudes and intentions of a deliberate murderer.

Yet Abigail refused to be dragged down into the ditch of his desperation, just as she had always refused to be dragged down to the low level of Nabal's folly and intransigence. She was a woman who walked on the high road of a noble and wholesome life with God.

She called David to remember his own great days under God's mighty hand. It was God who had chosen and anointed him to become a monarch in Israel. It was in God's service that he had fought such heroic battles against Goliath and the Philistines. It was God who had bound up his life as a special intimate treasure in His own possession. It was God who would preserve him from his enemies and establish his regency in Israel.

With such noble prospects before him, surely David did not wish to have his conscience stained with the memory of needless bloodshed in this moment of anger. Let God be God! Let Him avenge his enemies. Let Him be the One who would exalt David in due time.

Such wise entreaties did not fall on a hard heart. Their spiritual validity dissolved and swept away David's fierce anger. In an outburst of recognition for her counsel, David declared that he had respect for her advice. Even more he was prepared to accept her as a person of unusual gifts, sent of God to meet him.

156

Her overtures of peace had won the day. More important still, they had won his admiration. Her selfless love had won his heart. So he bade her go in peace. She had spared her family and saved him from great sin.

Little did either Abigail or David even dream that this dramatic first encounter was but a brief ten days away from Nabal's sudden death. What they had done had been done in sincerity, simplicity, integrity and innocence.

In the providential arrangements of the Almighty, this had been the prelude to a lifelong marriage. Out of apparent disaster God had brought a beautiful lifemate to David, His servant.

21
David Spares Saul a Second Time

Despite the implicit compact made between Saul and David at the cave where he cut off the royal robe, the latter did not trust the king. Saul's attitudes and actions had been as fickle and unpredictable as the untamed desert winds.

Over and over Saul had been seized with a sudden consuming passion to destroy David. Again and again he attacked in anger and black jealousy. His promises to spare the younger man's life were as empty as the summer clouds that evaporated to nothing over the hot sands.

Saul was simply not to be trusted. He had absolutely no credibility either with God or man. His word had no worth. He was totally dishonest.

For this reason above all others David remained a fugitive in the wilderness wastes. Yet from time to time, people still loyal to Saul would alert the king to David's whereabouts. They seemed to feel that by doing the tyrant king such favors somehow they could gain advantage for themselves.

Once again the Ziphites sent word that David was in the desert of Jeshimon. The first time Saul hunted him here he escaped only because of an unexpected invasion by the Philistines. So Saul had to cut short his pursuit. Now perhaps a second time, in the same desert hills, the king would succeed.

David sent out spies to reconnoiter the movements of Saul's army. As before, the king came armed with 3,000 warriors under Abner, bent on capturing David.

The action only confirmed David's deep intuition. Saul was determined to destroy him. The monarch's madness would drive him to the most despicable ends.

As an act of fearless courage David decided the time had come to prove once and for all that he and Saul were two totally different men. He wanted not only the armed forces of Israel, but also the entire nation to recognize the fact that Saul could not be trusted, whereas he, David, was a man of his word. It was essential for the future leadership of the people that they discover now how reliable David was.

That night he called for a volunteer from among his men to accompany him on a most daring mission. The two would go down into the very heart of Saul's camp under cover of darkness. They would be courting death. Slipping into the innermost ranks of the enemy, they would defy the overwhelming might of the monarch.

Abishai, a bold young lion, brother to Joab, David's second in command, stepped forward. He would accept the challenge and accompany his leader.

Like two stealthy leopards, David and Abishai stole softly through the night. They passed the outer circle of men on guard. Stepping silently they worked their way into the very heart of the huge encampment. So silent and skilled was their stalk that not a single soldier stirred. The two men came to where Saul lay stretched on the warm sand, surrounded on every side by fully armed men under Abner's command.

It was a typical military tactic for men to take their stations in a circle this way. Thus they surrounded their sovereign like the spokes of a wheel around a hub.

Because of his size and huge bulk it was easy to distinguish Saul asleep. His enormous spear, symbol of his power and manhood, was plunged in the warm sand by his bolster. Beside it stood his container of water so essential to survival in the desert heat.

The sight of the prostrate king lying at their very feet beneath the eerie glow of the sharp desert stars sent a shiver of excitement up Abishai's spine. Here was the enemy in his hand. Excitedly he whispered to David, *"God has delivered our enemy to you! Let me plunge this spear through his chest and pin him to the soil. I won't need to strike twice!"* (see v. 8).

David stretched out his strong arm and laid his warm hand on the young warrior's shoulder to calm him. *"No, Abishai, do not destroy him. You dare not stretch your arm against God's anointed one and be guiltless"* (see v. 9).

Slowly Abishai lowered the spear gripped in his hand only a few feet above Saul's wretched heart.

David whispered a few short phrases to his surprised young stalwart: *"I will not raise my hand against the Lord's chosen one. But grab his spear and water bottle. Let's go!"* (see v. 11).

As silently as two wraiths of smoke drifting from the dying campfires, the two men slipped back out through the sleeping soldiers. Not a single man stirred A deep sleep of providential origin engulfed the whole camp. For David it was a clean getaway, a total triumph.

It is worthy of note that David faced the very same formidable temptation in the dim darkness of this desert camp he had faced in the darkness of the cave. Both times his adversary was within easy reach of his weapons. Both times Saul's heart was but a few beats away from death. Both times the men with David urged him to destroy the adversary within his power.

Yet the marvel of it all was that the Spirit of God was sufficiently active in David's spirit to spare him from spilling Saul's blood. Somehow David, tough and formidable a warrior as he was, allowed his conscience, emotions and bodily reflexes to be controlled by the power of the Almighty. Despite the subtle suggestions of his fighting comrades, he simply would not succumb to their insistence that it was God's will for him to take Saul's life.

Quite obviously the circumstances which had put Saul so clearly into David's hand were arranged of the Most High. Still that did not give him either the license or the liberty to sin in avenging himself of all the wrongs perpetrated against him. Whatever final settling of the score was done would be accomplished by God.

In fact, David had made this very clear to Abishai in the midst of the camp. At the very moment of truth when Abishai stood over Saul's prostrate form asleep on the sand, his spear raised, ready to plunge it through his chest, David had warned him: *"Either the Lord will smite him, or he will die naturally, or perish in battle"* (see v. 10).

It was a profound statement, prophetic in content.

More than that, God would honor David in due time for not taking his revenge. The monarchy would pass to him. He would ultimately raise Israel to power and influence all across the Middle East, and David's name would become exalted above his fondest hopes.

Many present-day Christians are remiss in dealing with

the matter of revenge. They, like the worldly society of their worldly associates, seek to settle scores in their own ways, especially through means of ruthless contention and reprehensible litigation.

It should have no place in the life of God's child.

In this instance David had demonstrated clearly that the deep contrition and genuine repentance of his remorse in severing Saul's royal train had been a pivot point in his life. He would never raise his hand to injure Saul.

The same simply could not be said for Saul. The apparent tears of remorse which he shed outside the cave had no profound meaning. He had never been changed in spirit nor touched in the deep wellsprings of his will. If he had, he would never have pursued David again.

Standing safely outside the circle of the enemy camp, on the crest of a commanding hill, David shouted across the dark shadows: *"Abner, Abner, while you slept someone slipped into your camp and stole the king's spear and water container. Wake up. Look, see, in whose hands they are!"* (see v. 16).

David's shout awakened the whole camp. Instantly sleepy-eyed armed men leaped to their feet. Saul shook himself and recognized again the haunting, terrifying voice of his opponent. That voice could sing sweet ballads and psalms of praise, but it could also carry syllables sharper than any spear, more cutting than any sword.

"Why do you pursue me? What harm have I done you? Here is proof in my hand I could have killed you tonight!" (see v. 18). The sentences split the star-studded night like fiery darts, finding their mark in the hearts and minds of all the thousands of armed men hushed in the dark. *"Yet you come out into the wilderness to seek a mere mite like me. You assemble your men to hunt me down like a partridge in the mountains!"* (see v. 20).

Saul knew he had been fully exposed before all of his

men, and all of Israel. Word of this dramatic event would sweep back into every village, hamlet and home in Israel. The whole country would know now for certain that, *"David obviously was a man of his word."* In startling and convincing contrast every citizen could see that Saul lacked credibility.

Humbled and shamed Saul cried out: *"I have sinned. I have played the fool. I have erred grievously"* (see v. 21). The words sounded so contrite, so sincere. But they were not! For again this was but the cry of wounded pride. It was the shame of self-exposure. It was but that expression of worldly sorrow that leads downward to death and separation from God. (Read carefully 2 *Corinthians* 7:8–10 and *Hebrews* 6:4–6.)

Saul, who had been so carefully enlightened with spiritual truth by Samuel, who had been so generously endowed with God's gift of grace in preparation for his kingship, who had partaken of the presence of God's Holy Spirit, had actually rejected and repudiated all of these divine benefits.

In doing so he had become a "castaway," a man hardened against both God and man.

Saul never saw that the evil of his ways and the sin of his soul were a crime against God Himself. He never saw with spiritual understanding that the stubbornness of his will, the disobedience of his spirit, the selfishness of his motives were an offense not only against men but an awful affront to the love of the Most High God.

Despite all that the Lord had done to deliver him from his self-centered preoccupation, Saul insisted on taking the downward path of his own self-destruction. God could not trust him. Nor could David trust him!

David called across the dry donga for someone to be sent over to fetch the king's spear and water cruse. He would not put himself within reach of Saul's arm again. He refused to risk his life with one so treacherous.

As the two parted, David again implored the king to refrain from persecuting him. Saul's assurance to the young man was that he was sure David would ultimately prevail and accomplish great exploits.

Yet in his muddled mind he was not at all sure this was so.

22

David, the Fierce Terrorist

Even though the Lord God had spared David's life again in the midst of great peril, somehow deep doubts and fearful forebodings began to impinge upon his spirit. It was as though a cloud of ominous uncertainty began to intrude itself between him and his God.

Instead of a sense of triumph commanding his conduct, David felt pursued like a partridge in the hills. Instead of believing that soon Saul would succumb, he began to be convinced of just the opposite. He was sure that Saul would destroy him.

In actual fact David said in his heart of hearts: *"I shall now perish one day by the hand of Saul"* (1 Samuel 27:1). This was the exact opposite of what he had told Abishai the night that soldier wished to plunge his spear through Saul's sleeping form. Musing in his own spirit, David went even further. He insisted, *"There is nothing better for me, than that I should escape speedily into the land of the Philistines"* (27:1). He felt there he would be safe from Saul's attacks.

For David this was a monumentally wrong decision.

It was to lead him down into the coastal terrain of the enemy. But even more important, it was to plunge him into a life of reckless terrorism that was the lowest point of his career. Not only would David's own life be corrupted, but also the lives of all the others who followed him with their families into enemy territory. He little knew that his hands would be stained with more blood and his soul more blackened by deception here than even happened later with *Bathsheba and Uriah.*

His evil alliance with Achish the king of Gath, the terrifying raids he made on the surrounding coastal communities, his total annihilation of defenseless women, children and even tiny babes, without a particle of mercy, his cunning cover-up of these despicable atrocities by outright lies and dark deceit, equal anything done today by terrorist gangs in the Middle East.

It is essential for us to understand what went wrong in David's life. It is not enough in a book of this kind merely to narrate the cataclysmic events. What was the major mistake that so twisted and corrupted his conduct?

It all began in the man's imagination. David began to imagine that the worst would befall him at the hand of Saul. He became convinced that somehow Saul would wipe him out. Therefore he concluded that his only solution was to seek refuge with the enemy Philistines.

It is noteworthy that in all of this David never once took God into consideration. He does not remind himself of God's faithfulness in preserving his life in the past. He does not seek His guidance for the next move. He refuses to trust Him to care for him and his family in Israel amid their danger.

David only looked at the crushing circumstances closing in around him. The result was to set his feet on a downward path of self-destruction. Instead of faith in

God, David was going by the apparent facts that led to so much fear, then foreboding, then fantasies and finally failure before God and man.

These are best set out in five fatal downward steps:

Facts—as they appear to our senses and minds.
Fears—that begin to arise in our emotions.
Foreboding—based on the foregoing facts.
Fantasies—false and deceptive imaginations.
Failure—to do God's will or act in faith.

This is an ominous process constantly at work in the lives of God's people. Especially is it true for us modern-day Christians who are conditioned by our humanistic culture and scientific education to base all decisions on fact-finding. Because all such data processing is determined only by our five fallible human senses, it makes no provision for the exercise of spiritual insights or quiet faith in Christ to overcome and surmount the apparent difficulties which confront us as God's people.

In the New Testament God's Spirit explains to us very clearly in 2 Corinthians 10:3–7 and in 1 Corinthians 1 and 2 how our imaginations should be brought under control to Christ. We are told clearly that the world's apparent wisdom is folly to God. Thus we are made to see that our confidence should reside in the wisdom of the Most High, *not in the wisdom of man.*

But all this David failed to do in this instance. He abandoned his confidence in Jehovah, then deliberately, in direct disobedience to the ancient commands of the Almighty, sought asylum with Achish. It was to literally join forces with the enemy. He was to turn his back on God.

The net result was to provide the enemy of his soul with a bridgehead in his spirit that would be devastating.

The result would nearly destroy him as God's man. When David came to Achish this time, he did not come as a single lone fugitive, scrabbling on the gates of Gath, like one demented. He came now with a fairly sizeable retinue of at least 600 fighting men. Because of David's prowess in battle and daring exploits, Achish regarded him as an asset to his own military might.

In recognition of this the Philistine king turned over the entire community of Ziklag to the exile. Here David and his men brought all their wives and their children to take up residence. In his misconduct before God he was now joined by roughly 2,000 of his countrymen. His wrong decisions were in truth leading others also into enormous peril.

For roughly sixteen months David's commune occupied Ziklag in comparative security. On the surface it appeared to be a rather clever arrangement. Saul, having heard that his antagonist and all his men had fled into Philistine territory, gave up the chase. No doubt in part this was because he had always been terrified by the Philistines and was reluctant to cross their borders in pursuit of David.

David, spirited adventurer that he was, did not just rest quietly in the calm security of Ziklag. Quite the opposite. He used it as his terrorist headquarters. From this redoubt he and his armed gangs swept out across the desert wastes toward the coastal communities occupied by the Geshurites, Gezrites and Amalekites. This region is now known as the infamous Gaza Strip.

David's terrorist attacks were fierce and cruel. Like a desert falcon stooping to the kill, the raiders would rush the villages slaughtering every man, woman and child in hot blood. Not only did the desert sands lie stained red with human blood but so, too, did David's dreadful hands.

No wonder that in the twilight of David's old age, God would not allow him to erect a temple of great honor to His name. For it would have been built by hands that had shed so much blood in needless passion.

The reason for David's ghastly and ruthless atrocities was that not a single living soul should survive to report his raids. Perhaps in part he had never forgotten how Doeg had betrayed him to Saul. So he made sure his evil deeds would not now be discovered by his enemies.

This ferocious and heartless violence hardened David's heart. Like case-hardened steel forged under pressure, it perverted his entire character. For, whenever he returned from his forays, he did not hesitate to lie deliberately to Achish about where he had been. He thought nothing of telling him that his attacks had been made against his own countrymen in Judah and Israel.

Achish and his cohorts must have been naive indeed to believe such false fabrications. But they did! In fact they congratulated themselves on finding such a formidable ally in Israel's exiled military commander.

David, of course, was using the terrorist attacks not only to demoralize his ancient enemies along the coast, but also to add enormous wealth to his own personal possessions. The first time he fled to Achish he came alone, a single fugitive, owning only Goliath's sword which he had commandeered from Ahimelech the priest.

By the end of his sixteen-month tenure in Ziklag he had become a wealthy robber baron, rich with the plunder seized from his hapless victims. His fierce warriors brought back booty of all kinds. They looted every community they crushed and came home to Ziklag with sheep, cattle, camels and asses. Loaded on the donkeys were piles of beautiful clothing, lavish apparel, gold, silver and other articles of value.

Why Achish needed to ask where David had collected

such contraband is hard to understand. All he had to do was see the style of garments borne on the camels and asses to know they did not come from Judah. Even a cursory glance at the brands on the oxen, camels and donkeys would have shown that they were stolen from the south. The indelible earmarks on the sheep were a dead giveaway of who the former owners were.

But Achish, like one newly in love, appeared totally blind to the glaring evidence before his excited eyes. He was so stimulated to have David as a cohort that in his giddy state he was ready to believe any fabrication. Little did he know what a fool he actually was!

So convinced was Achish that David had turned traitor to his own people, he even counted on him to go with him into battle against Israel. The Philistines were now planning a new attack on Saul and his army. Surely David would be more than willing to wage war against his former antagonist and oppressor.

Surprisingly David had sunk to such depths of self-degradation that he agreed to the suggestion. He assured Achish, *"Surely thou shalt know what thy servant can do"* (1 Samuel 28:1). It was a double-tongued statement. At this stage of his catastrophic career, who could possibly predict what David might do? Who could tell where he would turn next? Who could be sure whose life was safe in his company?

But Achish believed him, offering to make him his personal bodyguard. David had plunged to the very lowest level of depravity. He who had been hailed as Israel's hero, the champion of the Most High, the one who had slain ten thousand of the Philistines, had sold himself into total servitude as a private bodyguard to the Philistine king. The wages of sin are desperate and deadly. David had become a slave shackled by his own submission to evil.

David, the Fierce Terrorist

As predicted, the Philistine kings gathered their forces for another ferocious invasion of Israel from the north. News of the impending attack terrified Saul, as it always did. In panic he sought guidance of some spiritual sort.

But Samuel was dead. Ahimelech the priest and all his associates had been murdered by Doeg. The priest's son, Abiathar, had fled with David. Where could Saul turn? He sought counsel from the prophets and from *Urim*, but all in vain. No reply came from the Lord God.

Saul had rejected the Almighty. Now he in turn was rejected. His sins and his iniquity stood between him and the Most High. (Read Psalm 66:18; Isaiah 59:1–8.) Saul was not heard!

23

Saul and the Witch of Endor

In desperation Saul determined he would get some sort of guidance from God. He was driven by mortal terror of the Philistines, now massing their forces on the northern approaches to Israel. He could sense that this invasion would eclipse anything the enemy had ever launched against him before.

There were two main reasons for his panic. The first and foremost, quite naturally, was the loss of David, his brilliant former commanding officer, to the enemy side. Word had long since come to the king that his former son-in-law was in residence among the Philistines at Ziklag. Nor could he be sure that David might not turn traitor against his own monarch in retribution for all the abuse suffered under his tyranny.

The second cause of his fear was his lack of communion with the Most High. Even though Jonathan was a courageous warrior with great confidence in the Lord, his hard-headed father had no such trust. He had deliberately chosen to exercise his stubborn self-will against the guidance of God's Spirit. He had flaunted the authority of

175

the Almighty. He had flagrantly disobeyed the specific instructions given to him from above.

Now in his extremity he decided to turn to the occult for spiritual insight. He could sense that control of the kingdom was slipping from his grasp. He would try anything.

In the face of peril men do diabolical deeds. Saul was no exception. He ordered his servants to search for a spirit medium, a witch, whom he could consult. Strange as it may seem on the surface, they seemed to know at once where there was one. In fact, they assured the king she lived in a dark cave on Mount Tabor, at a spot known as Endor.

This was less than ten miles from where Saul had set up his military base in anticipation of meeting the Philistines in battle. Ancient tradition has it that this woman was actually Abner's mother—that her life had been spared because Abner was Saul's favorite army commander. She still lived, even though early in his reign the king had made a half-hearted attempt to eradicate all the spirit mediums from the nation, this being the express edict of the Lord God.

Disguising himself and accompanied by two men, Saul slipped away in the dark of night to meet her. He was supposed to be not only Israel's monarch, but also the spiritual leader of the nation. But he had sunk to the lowest level of primitive superstition. He had gravitated to the occult which had been so strictly forbidden to the chosen people of God.

The witch, who all her life had dealt in deception, was immediately on her guard. She had no intention of being trapped by this stranger in the night. No doubt the man's huge bulk, even though dressed in mufti, may have made her suspicious it was Saul himself. She well knew how often he had double-crossed David. Why not she?

In an outburst of supposed sincerity, Saul swore by Jehovah God that no harm would come to her. All he wanted, and wanted at once, was a word of guidance from Samuel . . . now long deceased. During his life the aged seer had been ignored again and again. Yet, now after the prophet's death, the contorted mind of Saul was sure the seer could foresee his future.

Before the woman could even begin her weird incantations Samuel appeared. He did not come at her behest. The prophet was there in person, as clearly recognizable as Moses and Elijah were later to be, when seen by Peter, James and John on the Mount of Transfiguration.

The sudden and unexpected appearance of Samuel shocked and terrified the witch. She knew at once she was in the presence of one much more potent than she was. She was in terror of Samuel, the servant of the Most High. He had about him the aura of God Himself. In terror she screamed with apprehension. This was not the usual weird apparition that came to her otherwise beclouded mind and deluded spirit.

This was an act of the Living Lord.

She knew that Samuel came with a solemn word for Saul. And in that instant she was sure the one who had come in mufti was the king. But he in his terror, stooped to the ground, his face in the dust of the dark cave, was utterly undone.

Neither of them had expected such drastic events.

As stated before in this book, *"Be sure, what you demand from God, you will get!"* Saul insisted that he hear from the spirit world. And he did—directly, clearly, unequivocally. The message Samuel conveyed shattered the bowed king. It was to be his last warning from the Lord.

In a few sharp, stabbing sentences Samuel repeated Saul's past and foretold his future. It was as if his entire lifetime had been telescoped into a span of a few seconds. Such is the capacity of those who live in the spirit realm, no longer constrained by time and space.

In rapid succession Samuel outlined Saul's pathetic and tragic record:

"1) The Lord has departed from you.

2) He has actually become your adversary.

3) The kingdom has been torn from you.

4) God has ordained it be given to David.

5) All of this because of your willful disobedience to God.

6) You and your army will fall before the Philistines.

7) You and your sons will perish tomorrow, to enter the realm of the departed ones" (see 1 Samuel 28:16–19).

Stunned and shattered by the pronouncement of the prophet, Saul collapsed. His huge form fell prostrate in the dirt. Terror gripped his rock-hard heart. Not a word escaped from his dry lips. He was like a log, lying lifeless in the dust—a tree fallen, cut off at the roots. Not a single syllable of self-reproach came from him. Not a solitary cry of remorse came from his anguished spirit. Not a hint of repentance came from his stony soul.

Without a doubt Samuel's sudden appearance was the final opportunity given to Saul, by God, for his repentance. This was a divine declaration to the tragic monarch of his alienation from the Most High. It was a restatement of his disobedience and willful rejection of God's purposes. It was an ominous warning of the eminent peril in which he stood.

Yet all of it moved him not a whit.

There was not a particle of remorse.
Not once did he seem to see the dark evil of his wicked ways nor cry out to God for mercy.

The end result was total destruction, not by the ordained will of God, but by Saul's own irreversible choices.

Throughout this study of both Saul's and David's lives we have seen them portrayed as men of mixed character. The Spirit of God in recording the events of Saul's tyrannical rule makes no attempt to cover up the weaknesses of either man. We see them both drawn in bold and glaring lines.

We discover their deception. We are startled by their brutality. We are astonished at their ruthless terrorist tactics. We are shown raw human nature in violent action. We become aware that only one thing seems to make a stupendous difference between the two individuals.

Saul in his pride and self-centeredness would not repent!

David in humility of heart and acute brokenness of spirit saw his need of repentance before God and men—always!

The consequence was that God ultimately set Himself against Saul (read carefully Isaiah 63:9–10 and James 4:5–6).

Whereas with David there was a constant restoration that brought healing and wholesomeness to his life. Only God Himself, in generous forgiveness and abundant mercy, can lift the fallen and restore joy to the wretched ones.

Read carefully Psalms 51 and 34.

For Saul this was never the case. He knew little or nothing of the glad joy of communion with God. His dark

179

life, his somber moods, his muddied mind, were a grief to God's gracious Spirit and endless sorrow to his morbid soul.

Even the crafty witch in her black cave could sense this. Nor was she slow to exploit the tragic situation. The enemies of the Lord's people never are. She was determined to have a banquet to celebrate the occasion, since from her perspective the event turned out to be a total triumph.

In her cunning she was sure she had deluded Saul into believing that it was actually she who had brought up Samuel from the dead. In truth, it was the power of the living God, the same power which raised Christ from the dead and enabled Him to appear and reappear to His disciples after His resurrection, that energized Saul.

Secondly, she had extracted a promise from Saul, that, even though she dabbled in the occult and practiced witchcraft, her life would be spared and her future assured. This was an enormous concession in Israel (see Leviticus 20:27).

In doing this she had actually succeeded, in her own perverse manner, in making Saul sin against God. Secretly she probably rubbed her hands in glee to think the monarch who should have been Israel's spiritual shepherd was in fact allied with her in evil.

The third and perhaps most important triumph for her was to see that Saul simply refused to repent of his wicked ways. As he lay prone in the dust of her filthy, dark cave in the hill, she literally gloated over his anguish. He was spent in body, shattered in soul, dead in spirit.

In her craftiness she knew she could well afford to kill the fatted calf tethered outside the cave, bake fresh bread and offer both as a banquet to the king and his servants. There was everything to gain—their respect, their gratitude and their delusion. There was nothing to lose, because at best, Saul's physical strength would be restored sufficiently for him to go into battle and face certain, awful death.

The depths of depravity to which Saul had descended can be measured by the fact that he would even accept her food. It was an insult and humiliation enough for any man to take food or drink from a strange woman.

Here under the cover of darkness the erstwhile monarch ate his last meal on earth prepared over a witch's fire, fashioned by fiendish hands that dabbled in the occult. He could experience no greater indignity.

The evil spirits of the underworld looked on and laughed. What a triumph!

24

David Rejected by the Philistines

During the time Saul was seeking some sort of guidance from God, the Philistine armies had been massing on his northern flank. Under the command of five kings, huge concentrations of troops had marched northward along the Mediterranean coast. Then, swinging east, they moved down through the broad valley of Jezreel toward the plain where Saul and his forces were encamped.

Battalion by battalion the heavily armed raiders marched on in rank. Bringing up the rearguard was Achish, king of Gath. Accompanying him came David and his motley group of roughly 600 terrorists. It may seem incongruous that one anointed of God to be king over Israel should be found marching in company with the Philistines against his own countrymen.

Yet it is a vivid indication of just how far David had drifted away from the divine purposes of the Most High for him as a chosen man. His self-assertion in taking up residence among the enemy rather than trusting God to care for him in Israel had finally brought the young warrior to the verge of cruel calamity.

Even the savage Philistine warlords, quick to exploit any wrong move in Israel's affairs, sensed instinctively that David had put himself in a desperate dilemma. All of them, but Achish, were sure that in the heat of battle David and his men might well turn coat and become a fifth column in their midst.

After all, had David not been their most formidable foe in the past? Was he not the gallant one who with only a shepherd's sling slew their giant Goliath? Was he not the fierce warrior who had slaughtered 200 of their men to win Michal's hand? Was he not the brilliant and brave chief of Saul's armies who was heralded as a hero in Israel? Even the women and girls rattled their tambourines and sang their songs claiming "David has slain his ten thousands!"

What was this Hebrew, and his men, doing now encamped with them at Aphek? It was a valid question. They had every reason to challenge Achish on the point. He was literally bringing their mortal enemy into their ranks.

It is significant the Philistine kings specifically used the name *Hebrew*. First used of Abraham who had crossed over the Euphrates in his move to follow God in faith, it was a term meaning *"the one who has crossed over, or passed over."* It was then used of Israel as a nation who on the night of the Passover crossed over the upper reaches of the Red Sea into the desert of Sinai. Then forty years later, under Joshua's brilliant command, this same nation of a separate, called-out people, crossed over Jordan into Canaan, their land of promise from God.

These *Hebrews* ostensibly were known and seen to be a separate people. They were a nation without gods of wood or stone or precious metal. Their trust was in Jehovah, the unseen. To Him they gave their allegiance in faith.

What then was David doing here, they demanded? He simply had no place among them. He was bound to betray them in battle. Send him back they must. Let him return to his place of exile in Ziklag.

So the controversy raged on between the five leading Philistine kings and Achish who had granted David asylum in his territory. For his part Achish felt sure David could be trusted. He had gone so far as to make him his personal bodyguard. He had been bold enough to let David bring all his contingent on the long three-day march to the north. Surely he would prove a powerful ally in action!

But the majority opinion prevailed. Achish was compelled by the other kings to send David back to Ziklag. They wanted no part of him at Aphek.

The name "Aphek" is noteworthy. It means *"the place of restraint."* Little did either David or the Philistine warlords realize that at this critical spot it was indeed the very hand of God, at work behind the scenes, restraining David from degradation. It was here the Almighty intervened to spare his chosen one from calamity.

Had David gone into battle the next day against his own countrymen he would have betrayed Israel, his people, himself and the Lord God. On the other hand, if he had turned against the Philistines he would have betrayed his benefactor Achish and the simple trust that this desert chieftain had placed in him.

Either way David's reputation would have been ruined.

So that same night, during which Saul was in company with the witch of Endor, David was in deep discourse with Achish at Aphek. In His own generous, sovereign way God was using the most unlikely persons to try and spare those dear to Him.

Despite David's protests, Achish finally persuaded the

reluctant warrior to turn back and return to Ziklag at dawn. No doubt it was humiliating to be rejected in this way. It may have alerted David to the somber realization that he really did not belong here at all. Perhaps for the first time in nearly sixteen months he saw that by his own willful choices he had moved outside of God's arrangements for him.

Achish was obviously sorry to send him back. As naive and gullible as he had been, he could see no chicanery or duplicity in David. In fact he went so far as to reassure his deceiver that in his estimation David was as faultless as an angel of light.

Such a statement stuns us! Yet it discloses how crafty and cunning David's terrorist activities had been. It reveals how deceptive David's personal conduct and conversation had been in company with this desert warlord. Here his record was regarded as being above reproach, yet it was in truth black with the shed blood of his victims.

He who had lived fiercely as a desert hawk, was seen to be an angel of mercy by his Philistine friend. From such duplicity and depravity God would raise this one again. Surely with God all things are possible!

After his dismissal by Achish, David must have found the long march back to Ziklag dreadfully boring. Yet the slow hours that dragged by in the desert heat gave him time to ruminate over recent events. No one who claimed to be a servant of the Most High could also serve the enemy. As Christ Himself stated so clearly, centuries later, one cannot serve two masters at once. And as millions of men and women have discovered across the years, God's people simply are not where they should be in the enemy camp. They don't belong!

As David and his men approached Ziklag, after an absence of about a week, they were shocked to see wisps of gray smoke rising from heaps of ashes where their homes had stood. The town had been sacked by the rampaging Amalekites.

Not a single soul remained amid the ruins. Every wife, son and daughter had been swept away into captivity. Not a camel, sheep, ass or ox stood in the blazing sun. All had been driven off into the desert by the raiding nomads. The hand of fierce vengeance had swept across the scene in brutal devastation.

David was tasting the bitter wine of his own terrible atrocities, facing the ruthless violence of man's inhumanity to man. He was being shattered by the same sort of sorrow that he himself had perpetrated upon others.

The astonishing truth is that even his enemies were less brutal than he had been. For at least the Amalekites had spared his family's lives, whereas David had been a mass murderer.

Little wonder that we stand back in stark shock to see what steps God will take to remedy and restore such a man. Few of us realize the depths of utter degradation to which David had plunged. Nor can we grasp the full grace of God at work to raise such a criminal.

Now in self-pity, remorse and anguish David and his tough terrorist comrades broke down in tears. Their cries of anguish and moans of mourning drifted across the barren landscape. Their wailing rose on the hot desert air like the lonely cry of a jackal.

Apparently all was lost!

Their wives, their children, their livestock, their plundered booty, all were gone.

David stood stripped.

He had lost his credibility; he had lost the loyalty of his men; he had lost his leadership.

In anger, flaming hatred and the explosive unpredictability so current in human nature his men turned on him. They picked up rocks, ready to shatter his skull and break his bones. They would spill his blood and crush his flesh for the vultures to feed on before the sun had set.

David was at the point of extremity.

There was no place to turn—nowhere to flee!

Only God remained!

And in the moment of crisis, that was his only hope!

In genuine repentance he sought solace and succor from the presence of the Living Lord. He sought the consolation and counsel of God's gracious Spirit.

For the first time in sixteen months David turned from his wretched ways to seek the will of God. He was driven to see that *"There is a way which seems right unto a man, but the ends thereof are the ways of death"* (Proverbs 14:12).

In genuine remorse David called for young Abiathar the priest to come before him. He would seek through him, and the sacred ephod, to discover exactly what God wished him to do. No longer would he trust his own terrorist tactics. No longer would he rely on his own wilderness survival skills. No longer would he depend on the strength of his own military prowess.

It is God now who must direct him.
It is God who must determine his next move.
It is God who must decide his future.

These are the hallmarks of a man who in sincerity and humility has turned from his own wicked ways to seek the face of the Most High. This is true repentance. It is the proof positive of one who is humbled in heart (will), contrite in spirit, submissive to the purposes of God.

From such a soul, penitent and bowed before Him,

the Lord never turns away. To such a person He extends pardon and restoration. To such He comes in compassion to redeem and lift up. He is eager to renew again.

For Saul this never happened.

For David it did! He expressed it boldly in Psalm 56 (*read this passage reverently*).

And the word of consolation that came to David was that all would be well. He would overtake the raiders. He would be reunited with his loved ones. He would recover all his losses!

25

David Recovers All His Losses

On the surface it would seem natural for David and his troops to rush off in pursuit of the Amalekites. But it must be remembered this was not as easy as it sounds. They were a broken band of men at this point. The loss of their families was such a traumatic shock some may have virtually collapsed under its impact. After nearly a week on the march they were weary with travel and short of rations. None of these could be recovered at Ziklag.

The morale of David's men was low. Some felt betrayed by him. Their impression was they had been trapped by the Philistines then humiliated and devastated by the Amalekites. They lost confidence in their commander. Some were even shouting for his head. Discontent and open rebellion rumbled through their ranks. David was no leader fit to follow. He had only brought them to dark disaster.

Now, under the supposed guidance of God, David was again called into action: *"Pursue. Overtake the enemy. Recover all!"* (see v. 8). This charge came from the Lord.

And David was determined he and his men would carry it through.

It is a magnificent tribute to the caliber of his leadership that once more he was able to move his followers into combat. He clearly understood his commission. No matter the excruciating cost, he would act on it. This was a bold demonstration of implicit confidence in God. For David was sure it was the Most High who would enable him to triumph again while recovering all his losses.

The Spirit of God can only direct the individual who is prepared to move promptly in response to His clear commands. Too many Christians prefer to stand pat where they are, afraid to move in compliance with the commands of Christ. They never get anywhere with God. Because of their complacency they never gain new ground or take fresh territory.

Not so with David. He was not about to sit hopeless by the heap of ashes that had been his home. He would not remain there wringing his hands in grief over his losses. What was behind was behind! He was determined to press on into a perilous and unpredictable future, sure of only one thing: *"God was with him. His word was reliable. All was well."*

The entire troop marched as far as the brook Besor. Here roughly a third of David's men simply collapsed in the shade of the scrubby desert brush that grew along the banks of the muddy watercourse. It ran fitfully part of the year, most of the time being only a chain of pools, covered with scum, from which animals and desert birds drank.

David decided to strip his forces to the minimum battle gear. Any extra baggage would be left behind with the 200 spent men who elected to stay and guard the surplus equipment. The remaining 400, strong enough to go on, would be lightly armed, ready for swift action.

Then suddenly a most fortunate incident occurred. David's men came across a young Egyptian slave, weak and emaciated, at the point of death, lying in the thin shade of a scrub thorn bush. He had been abandoned in cruel unconcern by his Amalekite master. For three days and nights he'd had no nourishment.

David's warriors, tough as they were, took pity on the little fellow. His face was covered with flies; his lips were cracked with heat and thirst; his eyes were blank and empty with the hopeless stare of death. They lifted him up, poured water down his parched throat and plied him with figs and raisins. It was a generous gesture, for their own supplies were so meager and in short supply.

The lad recovered enough to be questioned carefully. Who was he? Where did he come from? To whom did he belong? In what direction had his masters gone?

He proved to be a tremendous asset—as we might say, one of "God's bonuses" in the hour of need. For when David promised to spare his life and not return him to his cruel owners, the slave spilled out his whole history.

He recounted carefully all the raids he had been on with the Amalekites. He told of every village and town, both in Judah and among the Philistines which had been ravaged. Best of all, he knew for sure in which direction the terrorists had gone and where they now would be camped.

It was a veritable windfall for David's weary men.

More than that, it was the special arrangement of God.

For, as of old, David could state fearlessly: *"I, being in the way, the Lord led me"* (Genesis 24:27).

The Almighty had proven Himself faithful to His own.

Again David had seen how emphatically God could be trusted even in the most dire extremity.

Always, always, *"Little is much when God is in it."* The smallest incident can prove to be a pivot point in life, when the Lord's hand leads us.

The key here, of course, was that the Israelis were not so selfish that they refused to share their own spartan rations with the stranger lad. It was a loving, gracious gesture to give him water and fruit and bread that their own bodies craved so fiercely in the desert wastes.

They could easily have deprived him of his needs and in the process impoverished themselves. Yet in the economy of God, he who is willing to lose his life on behalf of another, is sure to find his own preserved. Such generous giving is one of the rare and precious products of genuine repentance. It alters the entire course and outlook of a life.

Before the red and flaming glow of the desert sun had sunk behind the western skyline that night, David and his men had come in view of the Amalekite encampment. The desert brigands, so sure of themselves, so heady with conquest, so bloated with booty, were celebrating their latest victories.

Campfires had been lit. The fragrance of roasting meat rose into the still evening air. The wineskins had been opened for a bout of heavy drinking. Stripped of their weapons, the desert nomads shouted chants of triumph to each other, danced around the leaping flames and made merry with their singing.

It was the crucial moment for David to attack.

Like a pride of lions leaping into a herd of grazing gazelles, he and his warriors rushed the enemy camp in the semi-darkness.

Despite their fatigue the 400 Hebrews fought with

fury. Not only were they destroying an ancient enemy, but even more importantly they were rescuing their own wives, children and personal possessions. The bloody battle raged on all through the night. The element of total surprise and sudden attack gave David's men an enormous advantage.

All the next day the unbridled slaughter went on. It was as if suddenly new life, fresh force and electric energy moved the Israelis to annihilate the Amalekites until not a single fighting man survived. It was a total rout and a complete conquest.

This was the very sort of action to which God had called Saul so many years before. But he had never obeyed the Lord. He had never complied with His commands nor carried out His charge. So once again Amalek had been a scourge to Israel, and now David dealt with them in fierce retribution.

As it was pointed out in an earlier chapter, Amalek always represents the resurgence of the old self-life, the formidable "flesh," which is such a scourge to God's person. Always God's Spirit is set in array against him (see Galatians 5:16–17). And He calls us to have the old self put to death by the faith of the Son of God at work in us.

This, too, is possible only in the experience of the one who has truly repented before the Lord. For it is only as we set aside our pride, humble ourselves and beseech Christ to enter our lives that He can overcome the enemy of "self" within. It is He, then, who works in us both to will and to do of His own good, great pleasure (Philippians 2:13).

The reunion of David's forces with their families was ecstatic. Men and women fell into each other's arms in warm embrace. Tears streamed down flushed faces as tough warriors, stained with blood and coated in dust, gathered up their children in huge hugs and burning kisses. Not a woman was missing, not a single child was lost. All were there!

What a triumph!
What a celebration!
What a joy!

In addition to this ecstasy was the incredible bounty of recovering all their livestock, all their possessions as well as all the extra plunder and booty the Amalekites had lifted in their raids throughout Judah and Philistia. It was more than the victors had ever imagined even in their wildest fantasies. In forty-eight hours total tragedy had been turned into total triumph under the strong hand of the Most High.

This David knew, and this he recognized publicly. It was God who had led them! It was God who had preserved them! It was God who had given victory!

When David returned to the brook Besor, with such good tidings and good will, to pick up the rest of his men, an undercurrent of discontent ran through his troops: *"Why should those who stayed behind share in the spoils?"* (see v. 24).

David with strength, wisdom and courage silenced the dispute at once. God it was who had given such an abundance. It was only fair and equitable that all of them together should have a share in the spoils of war. Both the ones who went into battle, and those who stayed behind to guard the battle gear, should share alike.

It was a most astute action. It immediately healed the breach between his quarrelsome warriors. More than that it rekindled the sense of loyalty and respect for his leadership that had been lost a few days before. In the economy and generosity of Jehovah God, the one anointed to be king over His people was again being reinstated in a position of power and prestige.

But this pre-eminence was something that would not be confined to just his comrades in arms. David decided that a portion of the booty plundered by the Amalekites from villages in Judah should be returned to the rightful owners. It was reasonably easy to identify which livestock and other personal possessions came from each community. So he saw to it that a lavish share of the loot which he and his men might otherwise claim as prizes of war, went back to the original owners—as well as to those who befriended him in his exile.

This was an unprecedented gesture of good will and generosity. Not only did it demonstrate David's fairness but also his willingness to share the bounty bestowed on him by God, with others less fortunate. God would honor him for this with enormous wealth. Even by today's standards David would eventually become a multibillionaire.

Yet beyond even this, David was forging bonds of love, devotion and loyalty with the common people that would stand him in good stead. His future was being grounded in good will, love and genuine gratitude.

26
Saul's Death

Unknown to David and his men, the day they left the Philistine camp at Aphek to return to Ziklag, the army of Israel would be overcome. In fact, for almost a week no word came to them at all of the fierce battles in which Saul and his three sons, including Jonathan, were killed by the rampaging raiders.

Suddenly, in a single devastating attack, the Philistines had not only killed Israel's king, but also his sons, who might well have been contenders for the throne. The princes, too, in Israel were slain. The Hebrews had taken flight like so many sparrows scattered by the attack of a Harrier hawk. At will the enemy hordes swept across the nation plundering and occupying its towns and villages.

Though Saul had ruled with tyranny and terror for forty years, Israel, at the end of that era, lay beaten and distraught under the heel of its ancient foes. No ground had been gained. No new boundaries had been extended. No sense of security or strength as a people had been established. In terrible truth it had been a time of great anguish and deep remorse for God's people.

The sequence of events that took place at the end of Saul's life have been recorded both in the last chapter of 1 Samuel as well as in the first chapter of 2 Samuel. In addition the narrative given in 1 Chronicles adds further information. Contrary to the view taken by some scholars, my conviction is that because they are the various reports made by participants in the heat and fury of battle, there is bound to be some discrepancy in the details, depending upon the individual observer's personal perspective. Combining these eye-witness accounts into a single narrative we must conclude the biblical accounts are accurate and authentic in their diversity.

When the Philistine forces attacked, it was not only with armed men on foot, but also with archers riding furiously in chariots. Israel had no match for these. Since the days of Joshua, when Israel had destroyed all of the chariots and horses of the Canaanites, the nation had never resorted to the use of wheeled equipment for combat.

Saul and his warriors were overwhelmed with the furious onslaught. Turning in terror they began to flee for their lives, seeking escape on the high ground of Mount Gilboa. As they turned their backs to the Philistines they became vulnerable targets for the cruel arrows that found their mark in the openings where the armor was fastened between their shoulder blades.

The enemy arrows did their deadly work among the Israelis, severing veins and arteries, cutting nerves and tissues, with blood gushing from the gashes made by the barbed heads. Like grisly pin cushions Saul and his three sons Jonathan, Abinadab and Melchishua stumbled and fell before the screaming Philistines. The rocky slopes of the hill were littered with the bodies of dead and dying warriors.

In his anguish and terror Saul screamed out to his armorbearer to end his agony. But the young man, awed by the fact that his master was God's anointed king, refused to lift his sword against the monarch. So Saul in a last melancholy act of despair tried to take his own life by rising up and falling upon his own weapon.

The armorbearer, aghast at what he saw, followed suit and took his own life. No doubt had he survived the battle, his own life would have been forfeit, for failing to save the king.

Just at this juncture a young Amalekite, who somehow had ensconsed himself in the royal household and was attached to Saul's camp, came upon the fallen monarch. In the confusion and carnage he heard groans from the ground. It was Saul in the agony of his death throes.

Looking around behind him Saul inquired who it was. The young man replied, *"I am an Amalekite!"* He was one of the hated ones whom God had commanded Saul to eliminate so long ago.

In gasping tones Saul pled with him, *"Stand on me. Slay me. Take my life from me. End my agony"* (see 2 Samuel 1:9).

What the armorbearer had been afraid to do, the brash young Amalekite was quick to accomplish. More than that, he stood on the corpse, his bloody sandal on Saul's neck, and stripped the royal crown from the handsome head of Israel's monarch. As a final insult he lifted the great muscled arm of the giant man and wrenched the gold bracelet from his massive wrist.

The crown and bracelet would be sure evidence to anyone that Saul had been slain. Beyond that they were trophies of war that proved he, an Amalekite, had struck the last blow that brought this wretched king to such an ignominious end.

Saul who had refused to annihilate the Amalekites, who had spared their King Agag, who had adamantly rejected God's judgment upon this enemy, had now been utterly humbled by them. The events of his black career had come full circle. Thus the closing scene of his life was one of appalling pathos. Even the most obtuse novelist could scarcely have arranged a more ghastly ending, or construed a more sinister scenario.

Saul was simply a self-willed, selfish, stubborn sovereign who refused to relinquish the rule of his life to the Most High. He rebelled against the government of God just as Israel had. He repudiated the commands of the Lord. He spurned the sovereignty of God's Holy Spirit.

The end result was total disaster for him as a man. It was fierce retribution upon his entire family by the foe and total defeat for all of his armies. Resulting in complete chaos for the people of Israel, it was the worst sort of humiliation.

For when the Philistines found the fallen corpses of Saul and his sons on the battlefield they severed his head, just as David had severed Goliath's head. This grisly trophy of their triumph they sent all around their cities and villages to celebrate their conquest. Eventually it was placed in the sacred idol sanctuary of Dagon as proof that Dagon was greater than the Lord God Jehovah of Israel.

Saul's armor, so great, so massive, so brightly polished, yet now stained black with his own blood, was put in the sacred temple of Ashtaroth. As their goddess of war and violence, she was the one who had caused her warriors to triumph over the sons of Israel.

As a last ultimate insult the bodies of Saul and his sons were hung up like four ghastly scarecrows on the hot brick walls of Bethshana. This community belonged to the blacksmiths, a group despised even by their own people, to which Israel had turned again and again for iron implements and weapons of war. These men were held in the lowest esteem.

No darker insult or more terrible scorn could have been heaped upon Israel's first royal family. The four corpses, bloated with heat, blackened by the sun, covered with blood and gore, now putrified under the onslaught of maggots and decomposition.

Brave men from Jabesh-Gilead, hearing of this, were heroic enough to steal across the countryside by night to remove the bodies. They still remembered the great day when, nearly forty years before, Saul with a flash of faith in God, had rescued them and their families from the cruel Ammonites.

The warriors of Jabesh-Gilead bore the four decomposing bodies back across the Jordan. There, in their own fierce desert wastes, they cremated the corpses. Then without royal honors or any recognition from Saul's own people, they interred the bones in the desert sand beneath a tamarask tree. This was the very sort of tree under which Saul had whiled away so much of his life simply sitting softly in the shade, doing nothing either for God or man.

While all these morbid events had been under way David had been on his return march back to Ziklag. Then there had been the pursuit and slaughter of the Amalekites who carried off his possessions. Finally came the reunion with his men at the brook Besor, with the ultimate distribution of the spoils of war among his friends.

What a sharply contrasting series of events between the two men anointed of God to serve His people. On the one hand, carnage and chaos. On the other, victory and exhilaration.

Precisely at this point the young Amalekite who had stripped Saul of his crown and bracelet came into David's camp. No doubt he was confident the warrior king, in exile from Saul, would gladly welcome the news of his opponent's death.

With a certain flourish of self-assurance he retold all the gory details of how he had found Saul on Mount Gilboa. He graphically recounted how he had spilled the king's last blood.

As proof positive of his daring deed he pulled from beneath his dusty robe the king's royal crown and his golden bracelet. Like the former Amalekite king, Agag, he was sure his life would be spared by an indulgent David.

But he was dead wrong in his guess!

Instead David was distraught.

In a gesture of unbridled grief at the news of Saul's death and Jonathan's awful end, at the word about Israel's defeat, David tore his clothes into tatters. In an outburst of mourning he wept unashamedly, and so did his men. This was an hour of dark despair for all of Israel. Never in forty years had the nation stood at such a low ebb. In agony of spirit David along with his warriors refused to touch food or drink water until after sundown.

Like Samuel of old, David was not content to let matters rest there. Instinctively he knew that if in truth he was to be the one to succeed Saul as king in Israel, he would have to take stern steps to establish his spiritual leadership as well as his political power among his ravished people.

The first move he made was to summon the young Amalekite before him. He questioned him closely, until he was firmly convinced it was he who finally slew the Lord's anointed. In one short, sharp command he ordered the Amalekite to be killed on the spot. The man's own testimony was sufficient evidence of his dastardly deed.

It was a clear signal to all his followers—and to all of Israel—that Saul's era had ended. Whatever God commanded, David would do. A new dynasty had come into power, one in which the word of the Lord God would be obeyed.

27

David's Last Lament for Saul and Jonathan

Saul's tragic death, so full of shame and ignominy for Israel, was a brutal blow to David. The more so when at the same time he also lost his best friend, Jonathan the prince, as well as his two other brothers. In a single, awesome swoop of the enemy four lives of the royal family were annihilated in combat.

With fierce retribution, appalling judgment had brought an abrupt end to the era of Saul's terrible tyranny over Israel. We need to remember that David was not the only man driven into exile by Saul's ruthlessness. So, too, were the other 600 men who accompanied David during his wretched life in the desert wastes. Besides these were all their women and children who fled wherever they could find refuge from the mad king's wrath.

Saul's dark moods, his black anger, his wild and twisted personality had brought horrendous suffering to many in the nation. It will be remembered how he had wiped out the entire priesthood of Ahimelech. Doeg the Edomite had been sent to destroy 85 innocent servants of the Lord along with all their wives and children.

207

For many in Israel Saul's reign had been a rule of terror similar in harshness to the tyranny of modern, twentieth century dictatorships. Yet in the hour of mourning all of these evil memories were set aside.

On the memorable night that David and the daring young Abishai stood over Saul as he slept in his camp, within a sword stroke of death, David had predicted that the king might perish in battle. As Abishai begged for the chance to plunge his spear through that great heaving chest David had restrained the warrior's fury: *"No. Destroy him not: for who can stretch forth his hand against the Lord's anointed and be guiltless . . . the Lord shall smite him . . . or he shall descend into battle and perish!"*

These were prophetic words, pregnant with meaning. Now they had come to pass with remarkable accuracy. Events had turned out exactly as foretold.

Yet David did not gloat over any of this.

Even more remarkably, he never displayed any delight in the demise of his antagonist.

It comes home to us with tremendous impact that even though David had been hounded and harassed by Saul for so many, many years, he appeared to bear no personal grudge against him. David had a breadth of generosity, a depth of compassion in his character few of us ever possess. In this dimension of his life, at least, he was a truly great individual. He knew how to forgive!

This is not to overlook his singular faults. We have seen his propensity to deception. We have been stunned by the shortness of his temper, its explosive power, its crafty cruelty. He was a warrior of ruthless violence in combat, a terrorist who spilled innocent blood and brought savage suffering to his adversaries.

No, David was not a spotless saint! He was not a shining

knight of impeccable perfection. Like all of us there were lights and shadows to his make-up. Yet revenge against Saul was not one of them.

So when the day of mourning came to an end, David picked up his harp and with the natural genius of his musical talent began to sing a last lament for the leader whom Israel had lost in battle. It is a deeply moving dirge, replete with pathos, yet noble and magnificent in its expressions of love.

It has sometimes been called, "The Song of the Bow." Not in this case because it was accompanied by the soft strains of music drawn by a bow from a stringed instrument, but because it spoke of the deadly devastation wrought by the bows of the Philistine archers who wounded Saul in combat on Mount Gilboa.

In fact, this was the action which convinced David that some of his forces in the future would have to be men trained as skilled archers. This would be a new departure for Israel, just as equipping them with horses and chariots would be a new strategy in military matters.

But for the moment David turned his attention back over the years of Saul and Jonathan's exploits. He could not separate the two from each other. Father and son had stood together in life. They had fallen together in death. Nothing had ever divided them—neither Saul's foolish oaths and raging jealousy nor David's friendship.

Again David called to memory the handsome grandeur of the two men in the early days of their young glory. No men in Israel could compare with the arresting presence of these magnificent stalwarts. They stood strong like two splendid lions. In combat against the Ammonites Saul had been fierce as a predator, sparing the lives of all the people in Jabesh-Gilead. At the rock Bozez his son Jonathan had routed the Philistines single-handedly.

But now the mighty were fallen.
Now the Lord's anointed were destroyed.
Now the flower of Israel had faded.

David's harp sounded out the sorrowful notes. His deep voice, heavy with emotion, begged his hearers not to broadcast the evil tidings across the country. He wanted no dancing in the streets of Gath or Askelon because his comrades had fallen in combat. He wanted no shouts of triumph from Israel's ancient foes because of their victory in battle. He wanted no reproach upon the Most High in this hour of sorrow.

The gentle strains of the harp accompanied his lament. There was deep disquiet in the poet's sensitive soul. Profound remorse ran through the singer's spirit. Anguished emotions convulsed his countenance. He grieved with genuine sorrow.

On Mount Gilboa there had come a dreadful disaster for all of Israel. On that awful day the shield of faith in Jehovah God had been cast away. It was as though Saul had never known the special presence of God's Spirit there. Though both Saul and Jonathan, swift as eagles, strong as lions, slew the enemy with courage, they in turn fell before the foe. Their days of victory were over. Their hour of power had passed. The sad chapter of their lives had closed shut.

Still, it had been a bold chapter. David sang on in sadness. It had been an interlude Israel should never forget. Her daughters should recall the benefits bestowed upon them by the royal family—the beautiful garments, the golden ornaments, the lavish perfumes. But all of those were gone now. The soft days of ease and luxury and pleasure were past. The moonlit nights of dancing and singing in the streets were but a melancholy memory.

The recollection of those times brought David to tears. His voice sobbed as he sang eloquently of the great affection he had known for Jonathan. His friend had been closer than a brother, dearer than any lover. The bonds between them had been stronger than any bonds of blood, their loyalty more moving than any marriage vows.

In truth these two powerful, fearless warriors with their formidable faith in God were one in spirit, one in mind, one in devotion to the Most High. No doubt David had often dreamed that when in due time he came to the throne, Jonathan would serve as his chancellor, the first minister in the realm. It was a private pact between them But it was not to be. Jonathan was gone!

Because of the dark events of that dreadful day on Mount Gilboa, David's lament was that the rocky hill should stand always as a stern monument to the dark ordeal. Never again should the silver dew settle on those slopes. Never again should the gentle rain refresh those heights. Never again should the soil produce a crop to harvest as an offering to the Lord.

For He, the Almighty, the Eternal One, Creator of heaven and earth, looked for more from His chosen people than mere sacrifices and offerings. He desired something from His children beyond bulls, calves, fruit or grain. He longed for their loyalty. He longed for their love. He longed for their simple, quiet, gentle compliance with His commands.

This Saul had failed to do. In stubbornness of spirit and waywardness of will he had refused to comply with the wishes of God. In deliberate disobedience he had repeatedly rejected the Word of God. With painful perverseness he had refused to repent of his rebellion.

The choices were his. The disastrous decisions had led to total alienation from Jehovah. His faith in God had been diluted to nothing, while he himself had become a tragic castaway.

Yes, oh yes, Mount Gilboa would stand stark and dark, unforgettable as a solemn reminder to all men of all time that the sinister wages of sin are death. No person can sin with impunity against the love and mercy and patience of God, without paying the ultimate penalty.

David's lament was, without question, a deep and compelling expression of his own spirit. It came as a clear confirmation of the profound affection he felt for Jonathan, and the reverent respect he held for Saul, as God's anointed king.

As those phrases flowed from his heart in harmony with the musical melody of his harp, they were more than the mere words of a mortal man. They were the divine dirge of the gracious Spirit of God resident within his own spirit. Only the generous, forgiving, loving compassion of the living Lord could enable any man to give voice to such sentiments after so much suffering.

But above and beyond all of this tenderness, there came to David in this dark and meaningful moment, truth from the Most High. Not only truth amid tragedy, but also counsel in the midst of calamity and direction in the midst of dismay and disarray.

God is always like that.

He is the God of all comfort.

He is the God of all consolation and counsel.

He is the God of all compensation in our crises.

And the word which came clearly to David was that never, ever, should he abandon his faith in God. It was the Lord and He alone who could be relied upon in life It was God who must guide him in the formidable days ahead. It was God, who, in His constant love and care, would preserve him for the great and noble purposes he had been anointed to perform.

This would be the constant refrain of His life!

Spiritual Reflections

Basic Spiritual Principles Brought Out in This Book

God will grant what you insist on. At no time will He override your will. The results can be disastrous.

It is seldom that the Lord can use those of great talents. This is because gifted people are so often proud.

Few of us will set our wills to do only God's will. Instead, we set our minds and wills on our own interests.

Sexual perversion in any form is repugnant to God. It carries devastating consequences. It is a crime both against man, one's self and the Spirit of the Most High.

Anyone whom God calls into His service He prepares with great care. He fits and equips them for special deeds.

The secret of success in our life with the Lord is to receive Him as Heaven's Majesty. He must be preeminent . . . *always!*

Whenever we are disobedient to the wishes of God, at that point we provide the enemy with a bridgehead in our lives.

Too often God's people endeavor to achieve God's work in the world, using tools and techniques drawn from the world. . . . instead of relying upon His Spirit.

Our Father is not limited by numbers in what He can accomplish.

God performs great exploits with those who are simply expendable for Him.

We take personal vengeance into our own hands at great peril to our spiritual well-being. Let God settle scores.

Jealousy is one of the most despicable of all sins. Not only does it damage others but it destroys the one harboring it.

God calls each of us to deal drastically with our old self-life, just as He called Saul to destroy Amalek. Few of us do! We prefer to pander to our insidious self-interests.

Deliberate disobedience to our Father's will always ends in disaster. Out of genuine love for Him we should be eager to comply with His wishes, happy to honor His commands.

The person in rebellion against God's best purposes is no longer of service to the Most High.

The paramount quality of character Christ seeks in anyone called to serve Him is a humble will, set to obey Him. With such a soul God's Spirit delights to reside.

Those determined to follow Christ at any cost may well expect to face opposition or ridicule from family and friends.

If we are to achieve great exploits for our Father, we must throw ourselves into His causes. Only the person who lives for a cause much greater than himself, truly lives.

Our confidence for such exploits comes not from human skill or technology. It comes from a quiet faith in the greatness of our God.

The Most High calls us to put whatever skills we possess into His great hands. Entrusted to Him they triumph. The conquest over evil is both His and ours.

Any attack made on God's child is an attack made upon Christ who resides in that life. The battle is not ours alone, but His as well.

Even under the most severe and prolonged provocation we are to remain steadfast. Our constant assurance is "Oh, God, you are in this too! All is well."

Christ can preserve His people even in the most contrived circumstances of life. He often delivers us through the help of friends or the wise counsel of those who walk with Him in sincerity.

True Christian friendship is based not only on love for one another but also on deep mutual respect and open honesty. This leads to long-time loyalty.

We are not to fracture families in order to indulge our own desires for friendship.

Fear in our lives eventually leads to loss of faith in

God. It is the root cause of frustration and failure. Such an attitude does not come from the God of all hope.

Fear can drive us into duplicity and deception for self-preservation. It is a downward path of despair that leads others into evil as well.

In His mercy and compassion, Christ will and does send us His messengers to summon us from our darkness.

Often those who have erred can be quickly restored if they confess their wrongs and repent of their wicked ways.

True repentance, sometimes called "godly sorrow," is seldom seen in our society. This is basically because few of us see that our sins are criminal offenses against a loving Lord. They are what cost Christ the awful agony of Golgotha.

It was and always is God's intention to bring people to repentance. The modern church merely brings people to feel sorry for themselves. The two are poles apart!

Repentance is a continuous process which goes on between God's gracious Spirit and the will of the one set to please Christ.

There is an appropriate time and place for each of us to be courteous in dealing with others.

Boorishness and ill temper do not accomplish God's ends in this weary old world.

The one who truly loves and cares for others will run great risks to preserve peace.

God, our Father, has endowed women with unusual attributes of generosity and self-giving. Herein lies their greatest charm. To desire to become like men is to forfeit their greatest grace.

As God's people we dare not let others deflect us from doing our duty to God and man.

It is a most dangerous decision to ignore God's wishes in our lives and choose instead to do our own thing. Such choices are often based on our own fears or false imaginations which are not under Christ's control.

Wrong imaginations can lead us to align ourselves with the very enemies of God. They may even induce us to resort to the world's wicked ways. Thus we become sinister slaves to sin.

In the extremity of sin, those who refuse to repent find themselves trapped. Then, even the occult, or false religions, will hold a strong appeal to turn them from God.

The true child of God can never be comfortable in the company of the unregenerate. He is a split person of divided loyalties and divided affections.

Yet, for the one who repents, there is wondrous restoration. God, by His Spirit, will "lift up" the cast down. He will direct his steps into new paths of righteousness.

God calls His people to press on, to persevere, to pursue His desires with all diligence. For such He will do more than they can ever ask or think.

The tragic truth remains that for most of us, *self* still stands as our own fiercest foe. Unless we truly deny our *selves* we cannot ever be Christ's victorious followers.

AMEN.

OTHER WORD PRODUCTS BY W. PHILLIP KELLER

Lifelifter Cassettes:

Forgiveness—What It Is and What It Costs SPCN 201–0158–733

Lessons from a Sheep Dog SPCN 201–0129–733

The Potter and the Clay SPCN 201–0135–733

What It Means to Receive Jesus Christ SPCN 201–0195–736

Cassette Album

A Gardener Looks at the Fruits of the Spirit SPCN 201–0678–001

Film

Lessons from a Sheep Dog